EIRIK JOHNSON   SAWDUST MOUNTAIN

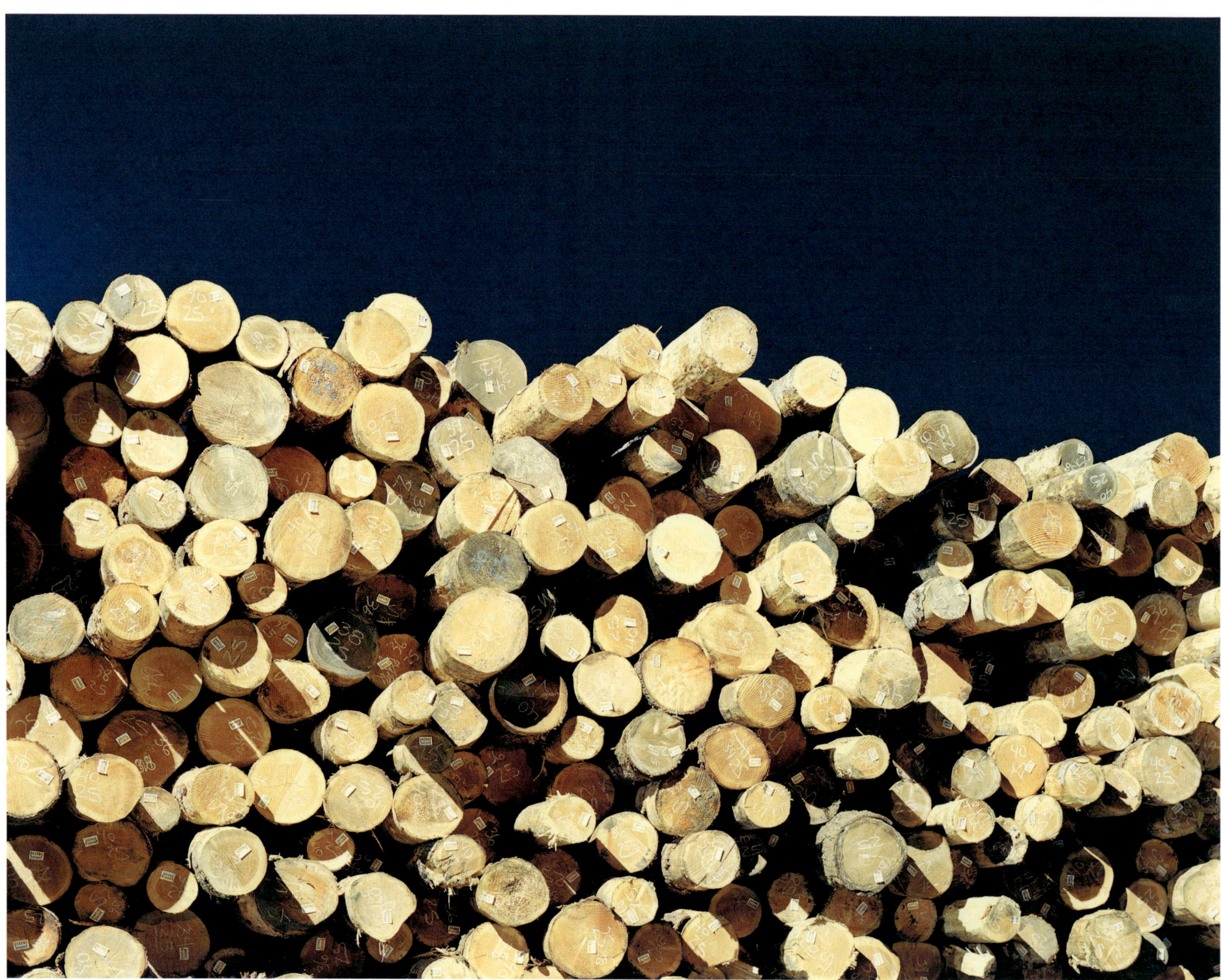

EIRIK JOHNSON SAWDUST MOUNTAIN

Foreword by Elizabeth A. Brown

Essay by Tess Gallagher

Poem by David Guterson

aperture   Henry Art Gallery

FOREWORD

Elizabeth A. Brown

The subject of *Sawdust Mountain* is a natural environment indelibly altered and marked by humankind. The ashen associations of the title signal the dry reality of a once-romantic subject. Old myths about the powerful, valiant lumberjacks have been supplanted by ecological critiques of clear-cutting, which destroys habitats and encourages erosion. Idyllic images of fishing—man pitting skill and strength against powerful, plentiful salmon—have been replaced with fears about the very survival of the species. Far from the nineteenth-century promise of bountiful assets awaiting harvest—which had drawn so many settlers to the Pacific Northwest—is the twenty-first-century recognition that natural-resource-based industries are not only finite, but most likely doomed. Even without exhausting the stock, economic concerns, such as transportation costs, or the efficiencies of mechanization, have challenged the viability of employment-for-life in timber or fishing.

Along the way, a rural population found itself cast adrift. The complexity of its condition is the subject of Eirik Johnson's endeavor. *Sawdust Mountain* encompasses not only fishermen and hatchery specialists, lumber workers, and reforestation projects, but also the disenfranchised: abandoned buildings and vehicles, makeshift stores only one step above yard sales. Some of the most touching images represent those creative, albeit desperate solutions: a Masonic Temple (originally built as an opera house) converted into a sweater store (page 89); the Art of Wood store (page 39); Just Sell It Now on eBay (page 93); Colin Sucher & Sons, a *Star Wars* emporium (page 95).

Formally, *Sawdust Mountain* represents a leap in Johnson's photographic skills, as well as a comprehensive tour of his influences. Earlier projects, such as *Animal Holes* and *Borderlands*, maintained a human scale and recognizable vantage point: close enough to see the subject clearly, broad enough to reveal its context. Breaking with this pattern, his photographs in *Sawdust Mountain* veer from near to far, including tight close-ups, individual portraits set in charged environments, and grand, distant views. In some cases, historical precedents influenced these new formats. Throughout *Sawdust Mountain* Johnson touches back to the epic scale and sublime beauty of Carleton Watkins's

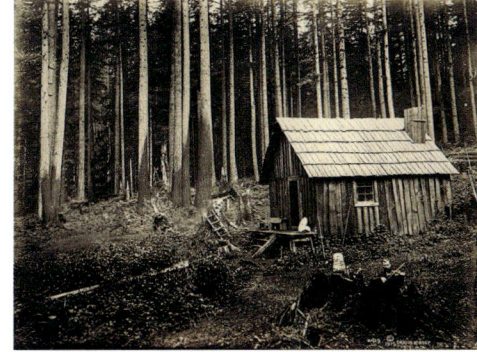

Figure 1 Darius Reynolds Kinsey, *The Fiddler (Shake Cabin on Homestead)*, 1897

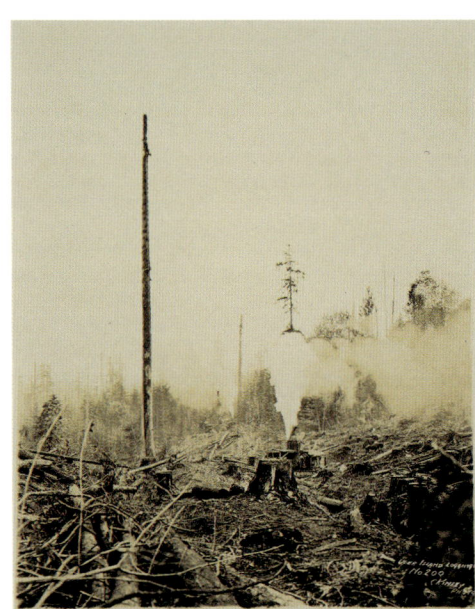

Figure 2 Clark Kinsey, *Deer Island Logging Co.,* c. 1913–1929

photographs, some of the earliest known images of the region. Such pictures as Makah tribal gill nets (page 109) and Below the Glines Canyon Dam (page 64) virtually quote Watkins, as long as one disregards the inconvenient traces of modern industry. now Johnson considers the Seattle-based figure Darius Kinsey a touchstone for this project. The Henry Art Gallery's photographs by Kinsey (1869–1945) and his brother Clark Kinsey (1877–1956) reveal traces of the timber industry in its infancy. Whereas Darius's charming vignette of a cabin in the woods attests to the endless forest in its virgin state (figure 1), Clark's record of a logging site suggests the aftermath (figure 2).

Johnson's particular use of color and of space reveals his close reading of several living photographers. He deliberated the specific colors of Northwest light in contrast to William Eggleston's Southern photographs: ". . . his harsh bright light and colors (dry and dusty earth, faded greens and intense blue skies) seemed like the mirror opposite of what I saw present in the Northwest," he says. I think of Joel Sternfeld when Johnson pulls back to view individuals in their environment, such as Carl near Sappho (page 113). Adult books (page 41), with telling details stacked up across space, reminds me of Stephen Shore. Robert Adams is an inevitable forebear, but Johnson thought less about his searing records of clear cuts than the ". . . flattened descriptive space between foreground and the distant background," characterizing Adams's LA photographs.

Sawdust Mountain is remarkable for the balance it strikes between these myriad competing concerns. Alternating pictorial beauty with surprising juxtapositions, Johnson found a vast array of subjects and moods under the Northwest's overcast skies, and developed personal connections with people at all points of the spectrum. One imagines him shifting roles with grace and empathy: anthropologist, researcher, formalist, hiker, storyteller, tracker, each facet of his formation establishing a connection to the topic at hand. Along the way he has established a new relationship with the land, the place of his origins, and has suggested ways for any viewer to begin to take in its complexities and its joys.

—Elizabeth A. Brown, Chief Curator, Henry Art Gallery

Closed Mill

Some of those trees are gone now and some remain.
The mill, evaporating, has left behind moss.
There's a skein of cable amid the blackberry
By the river—in the interstices of thorns,
Seized chokers, a seized engine.
Even the sawdust mountain's blown to weeds
Where there's no evading nettles any longer.
I remember the morning the cook
Quit, leaving his crumpled apron
Beneath warming lamps while slabs of french toast
Smoked on the griddle. I made enough enemies
To color the future. I didn't do anything to
Get off the wheel. My friend wanted
Jack Daniel's in the hospital and got it.
Someone tried to hit me with a hammer.
There was nowhere to go and we went
There together. Returning's no worse than
A bad dream, I think—but I'm remorseful,
Now, about that running mill.
All those trees pushed loudly through the saw
In the era when I was king.

—David Guterson

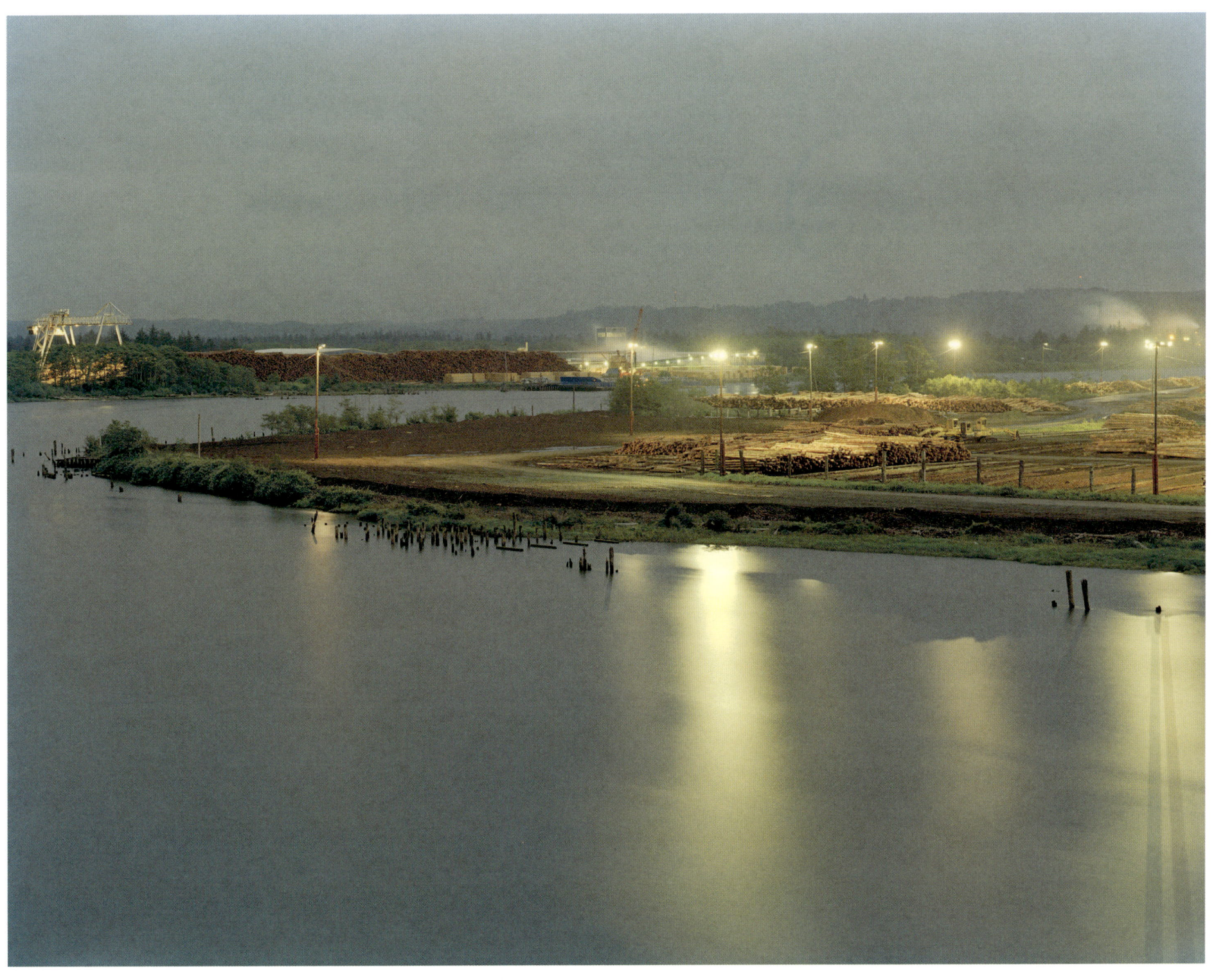

Weyerhaeuser sorting yard along the Chehalis River, Cosmopolis, Washington   11

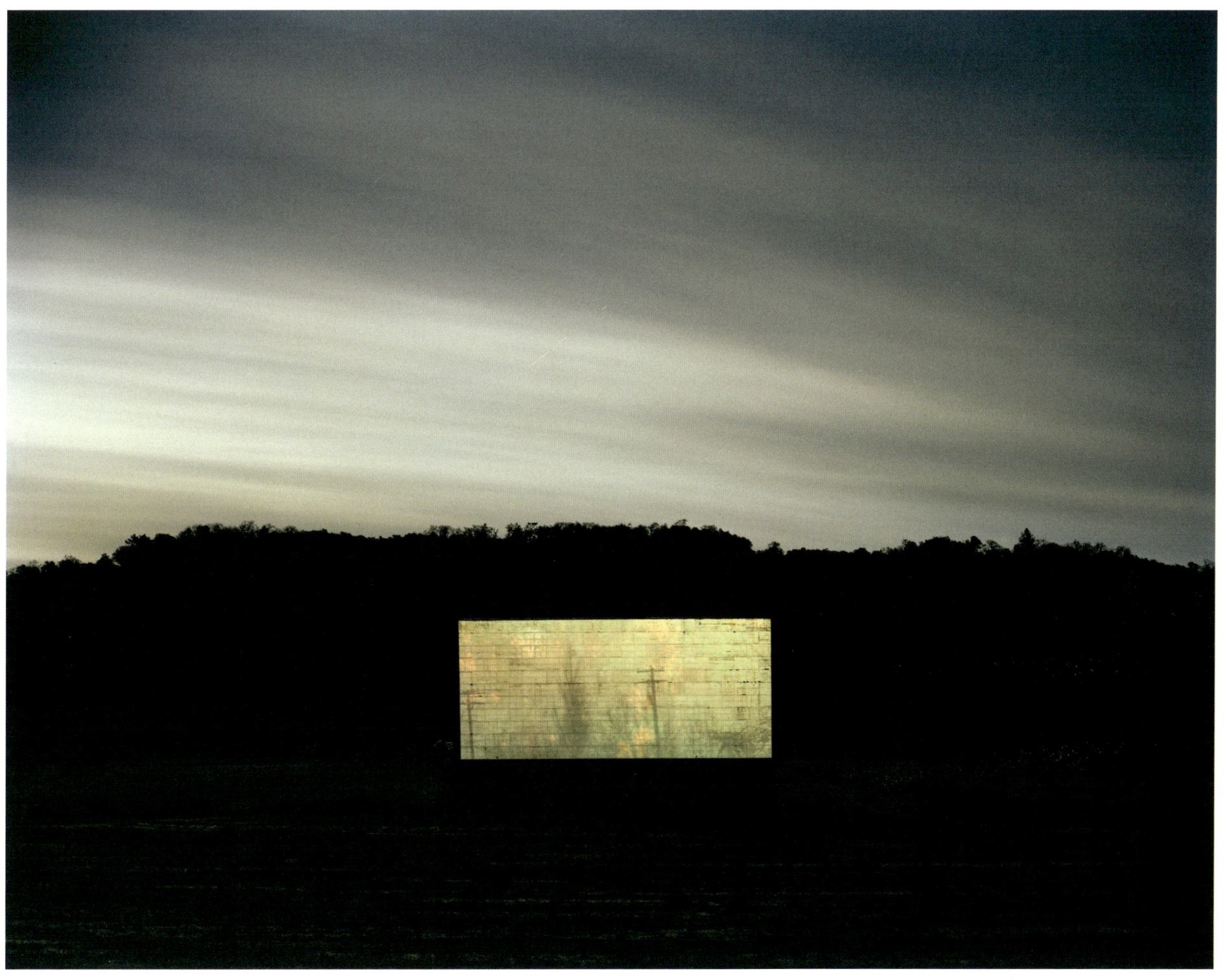

Starlite Drive-In, Roseburg, Oregon   13

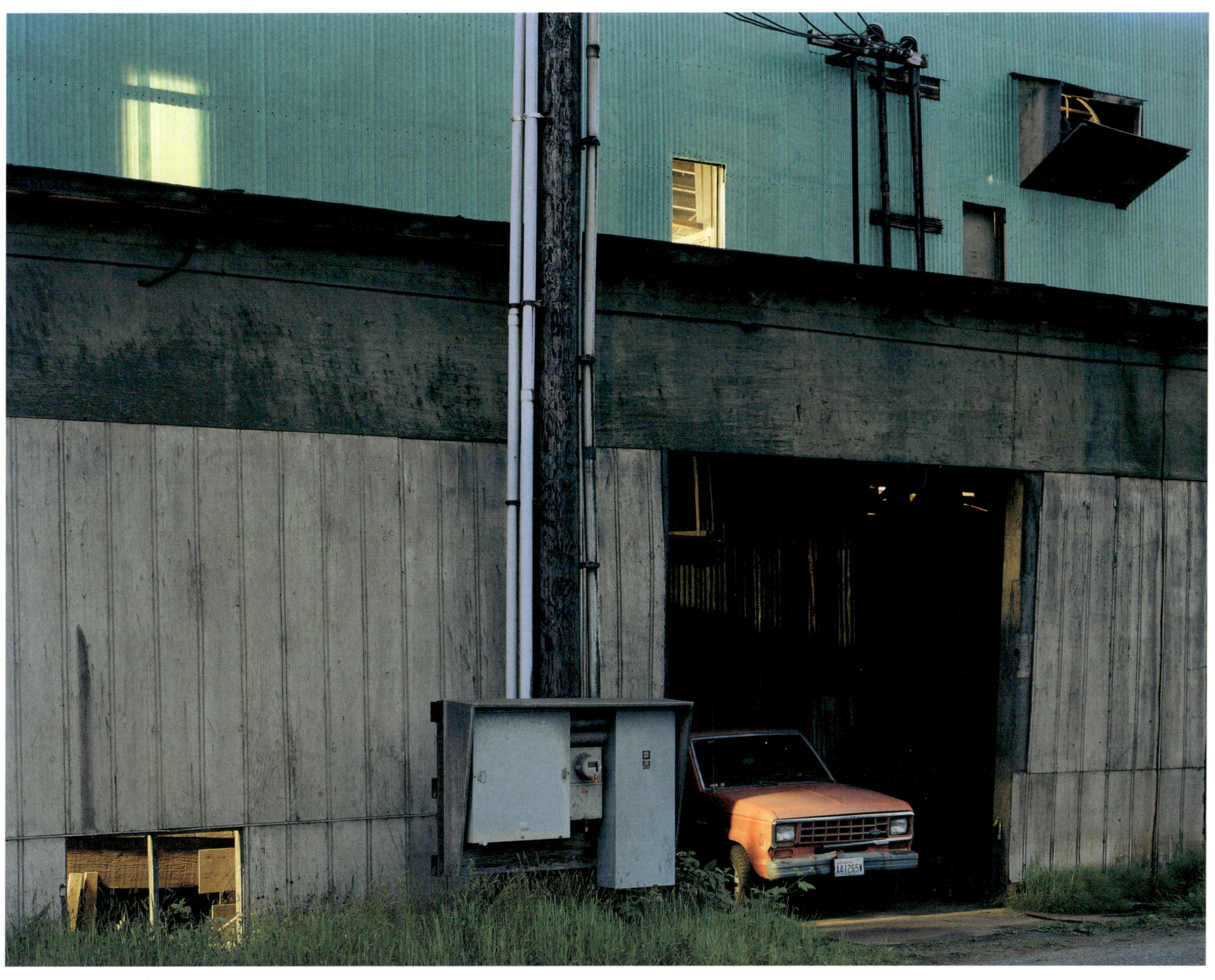

Mill, Aberdeen, Washington   15

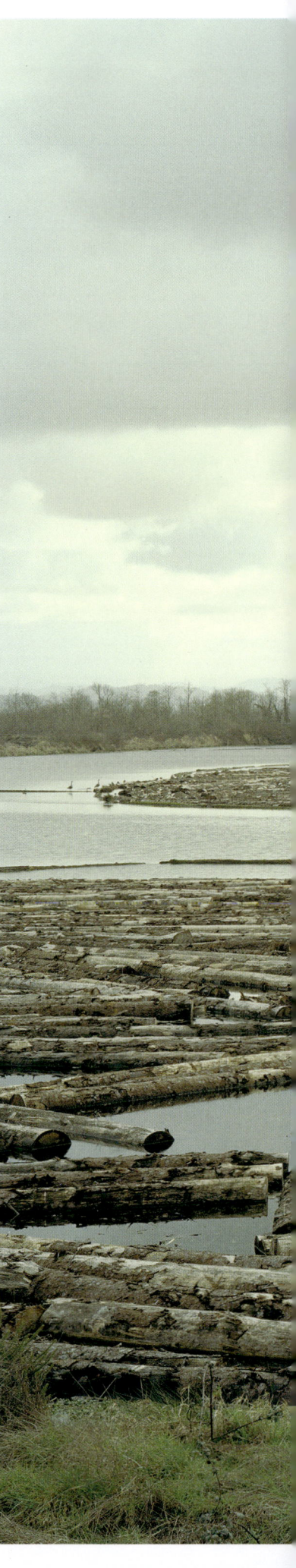

16   Coquille River, Oregon

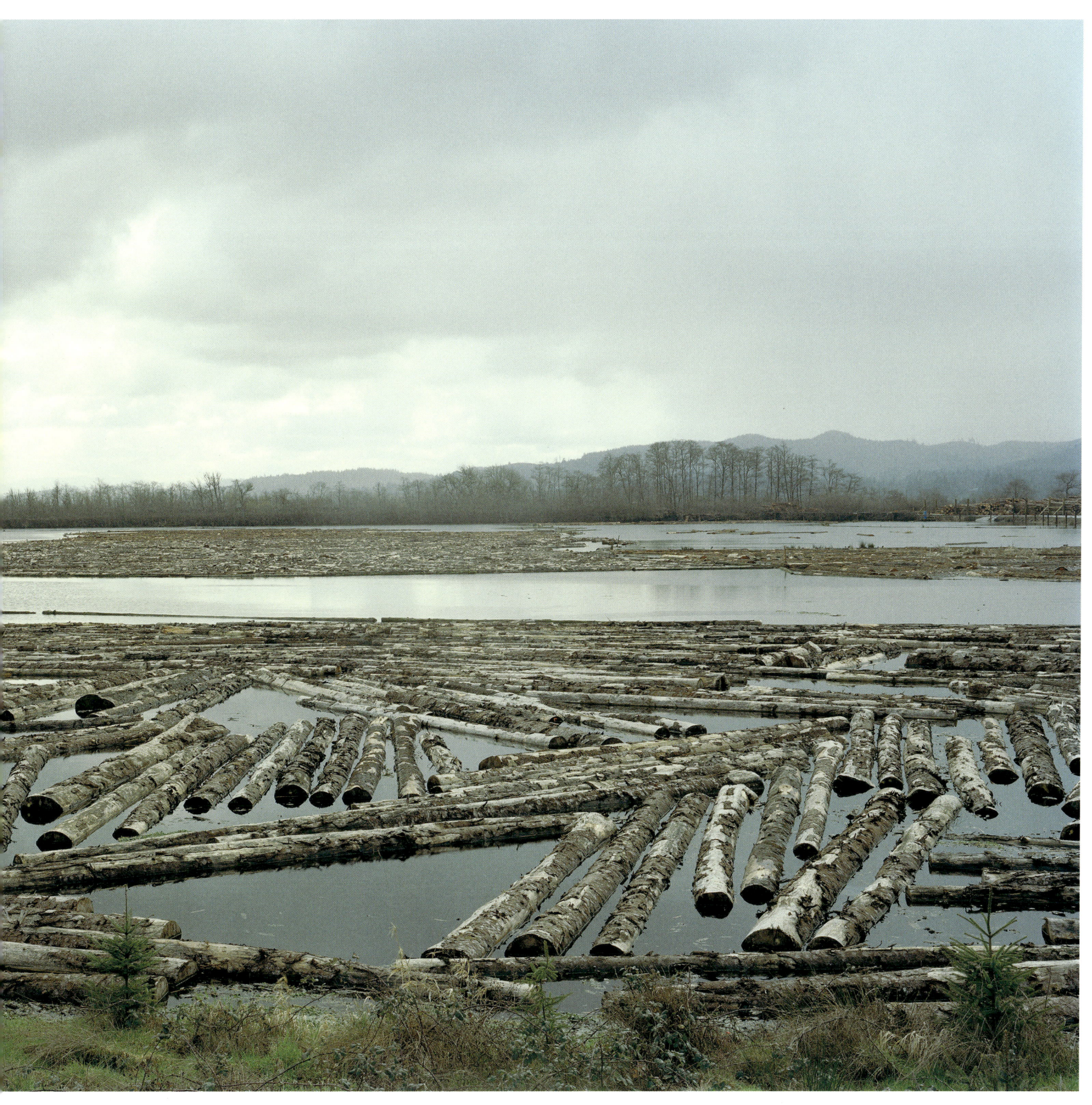

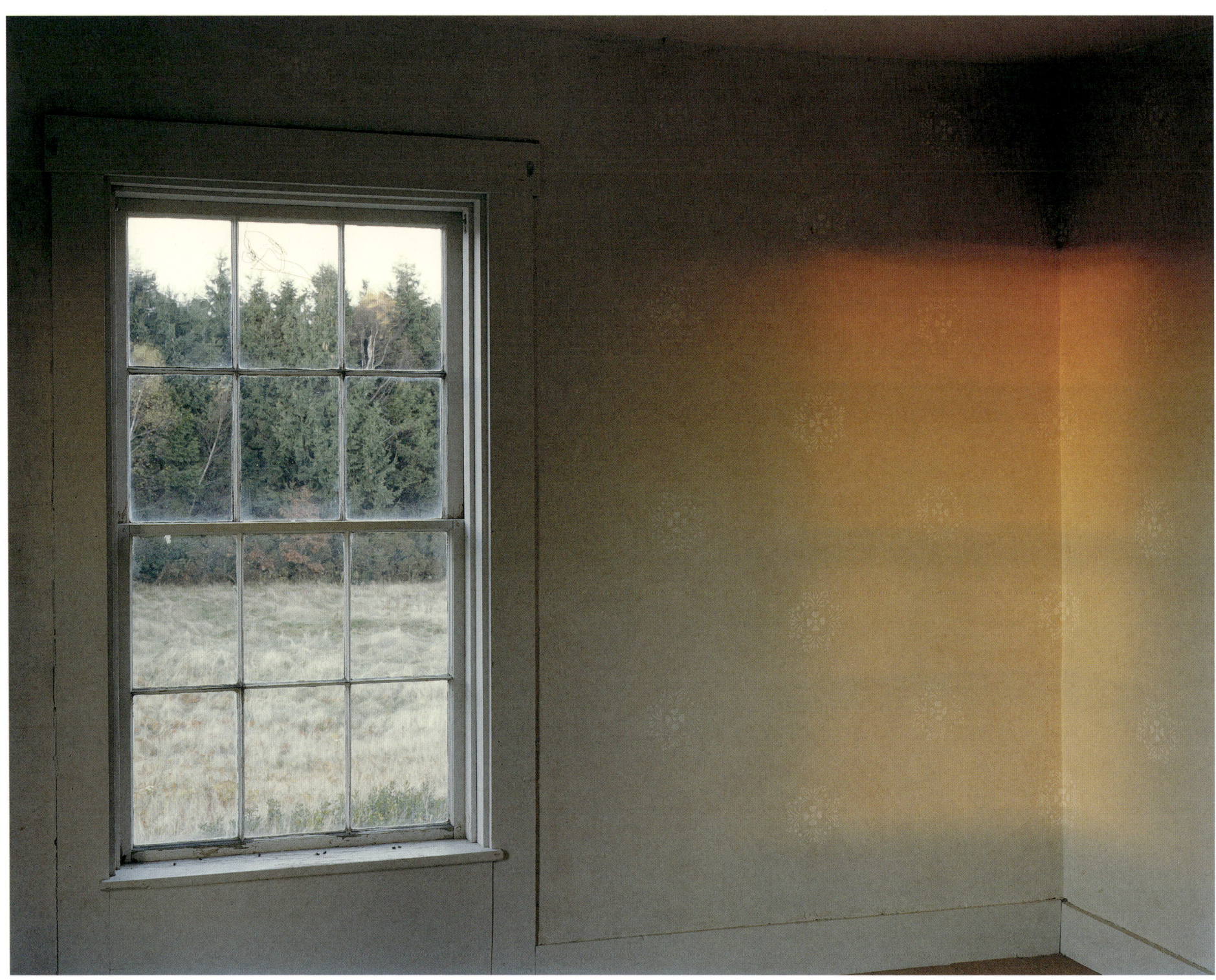

18   Coquille, Oregon

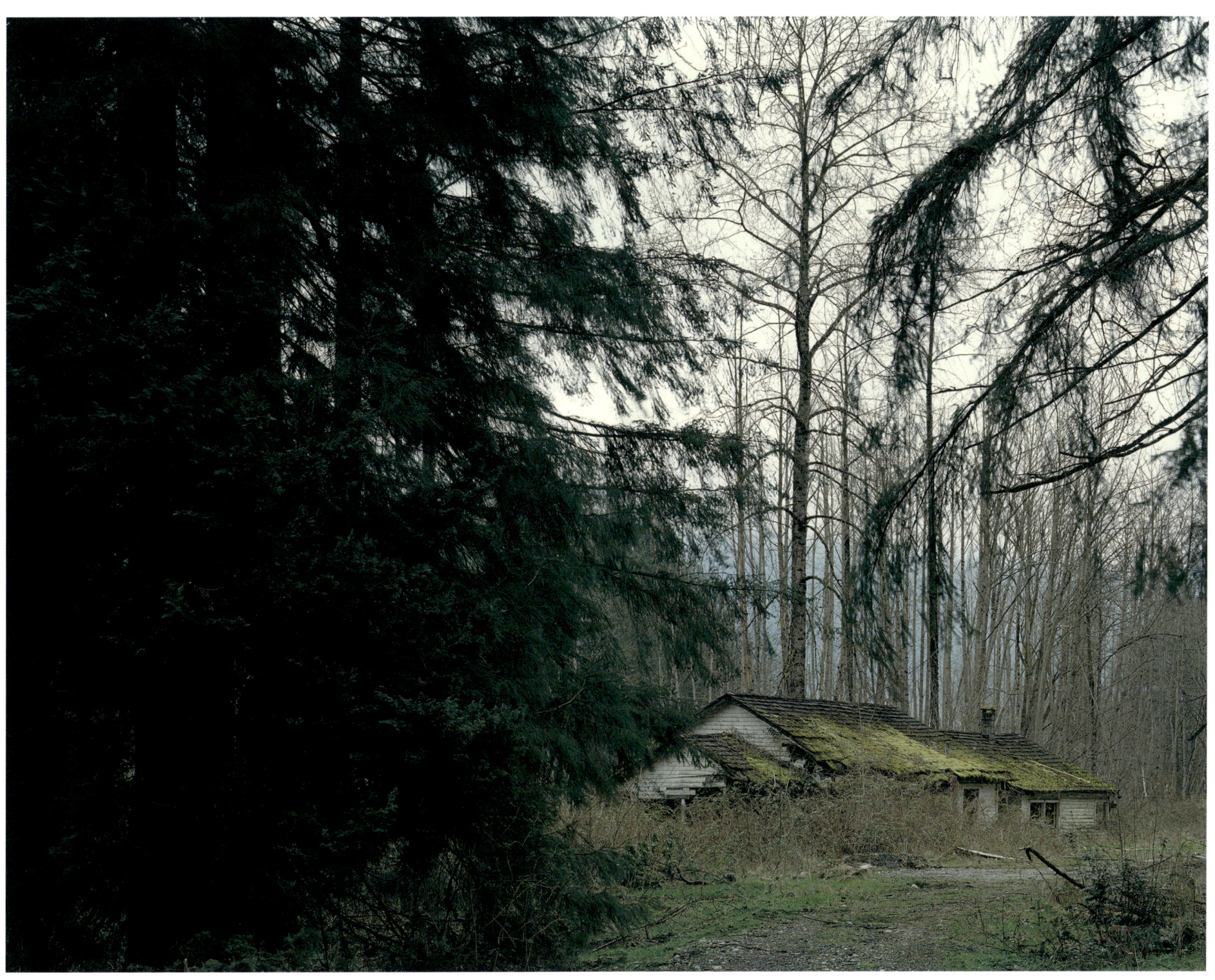

Arlington, Washington   19

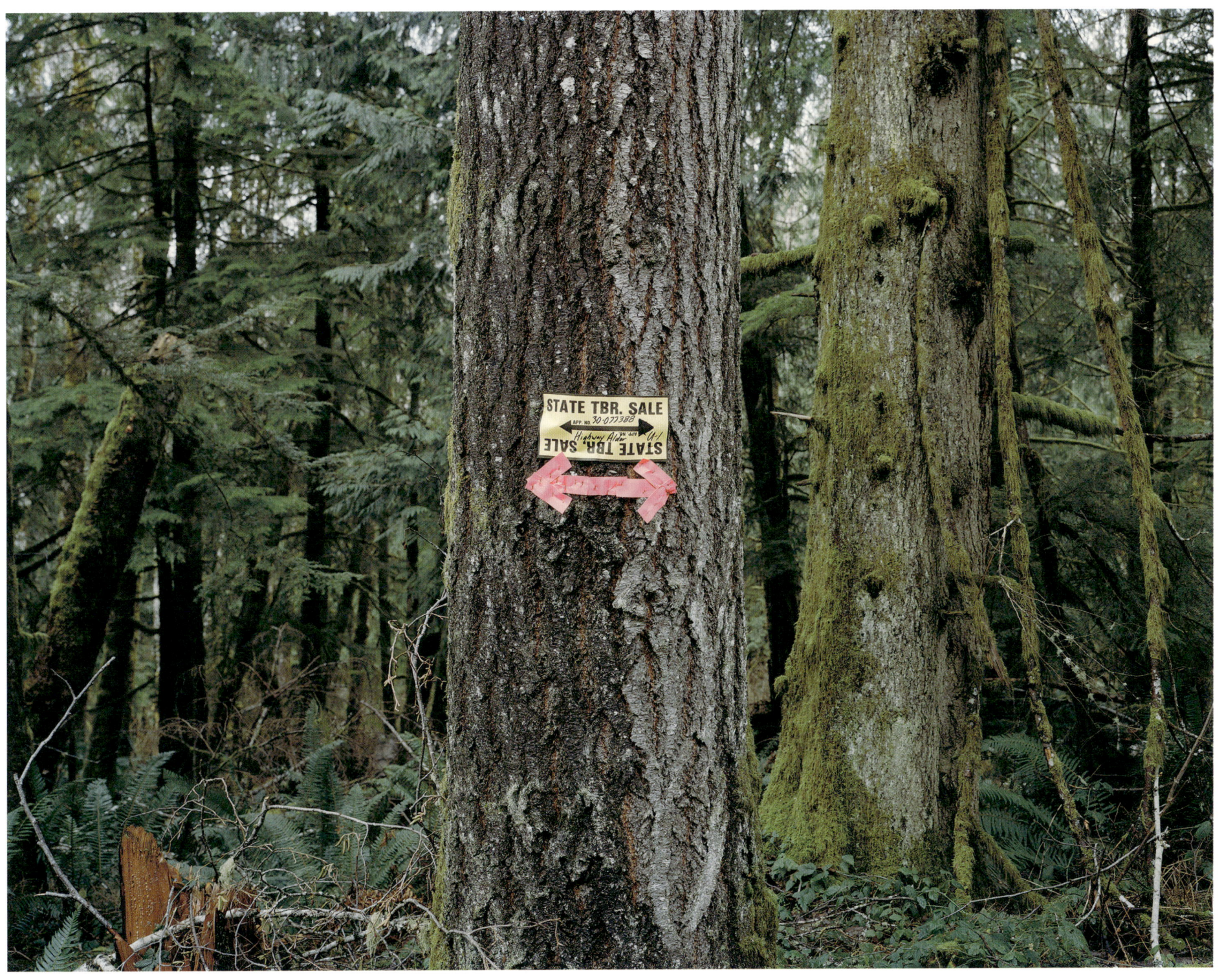

Timber for sale outside Clallam Bay, Washington   21

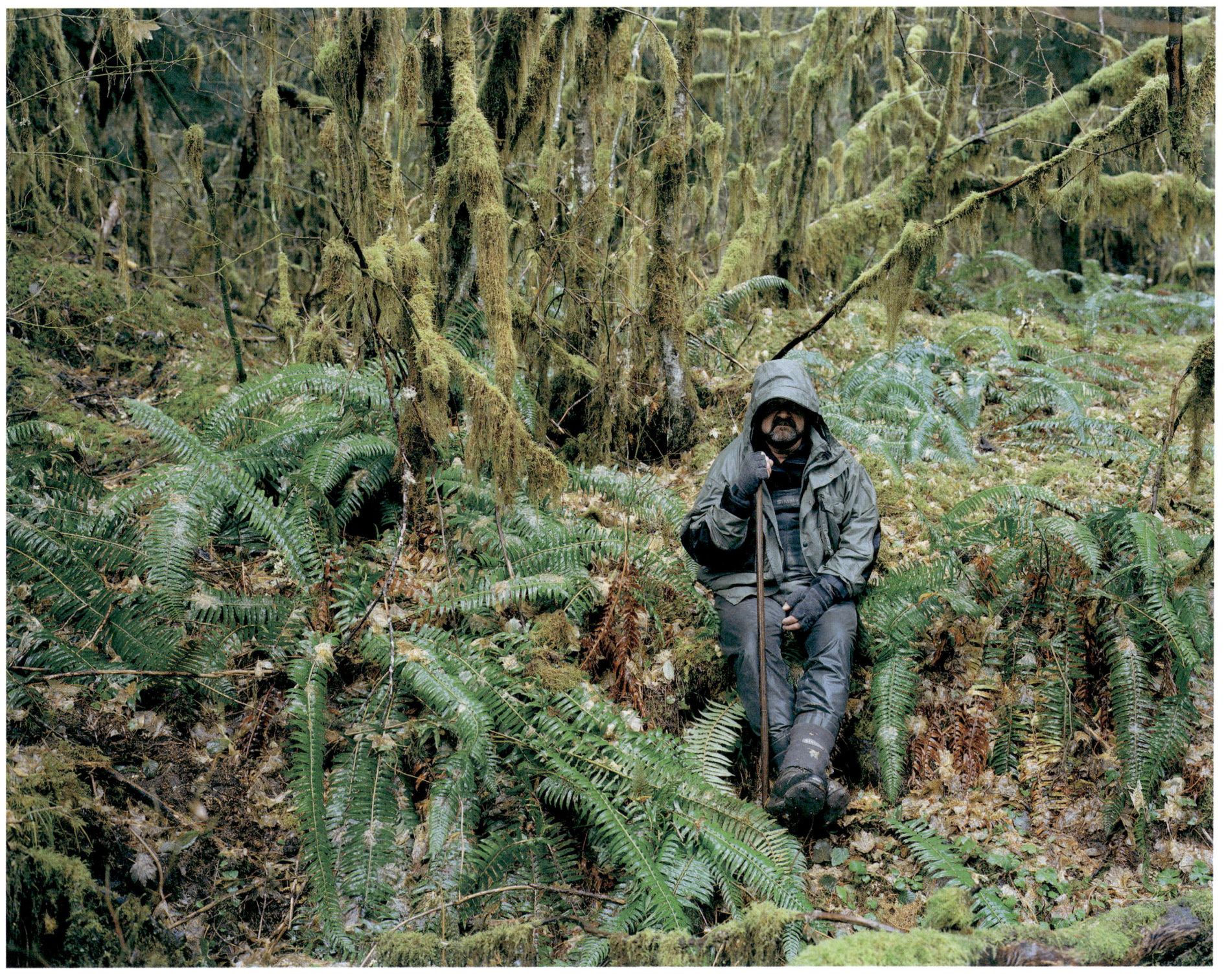

Roger Mosley counting Coho spawn nests along the upper Sol Duc River, Washington   23

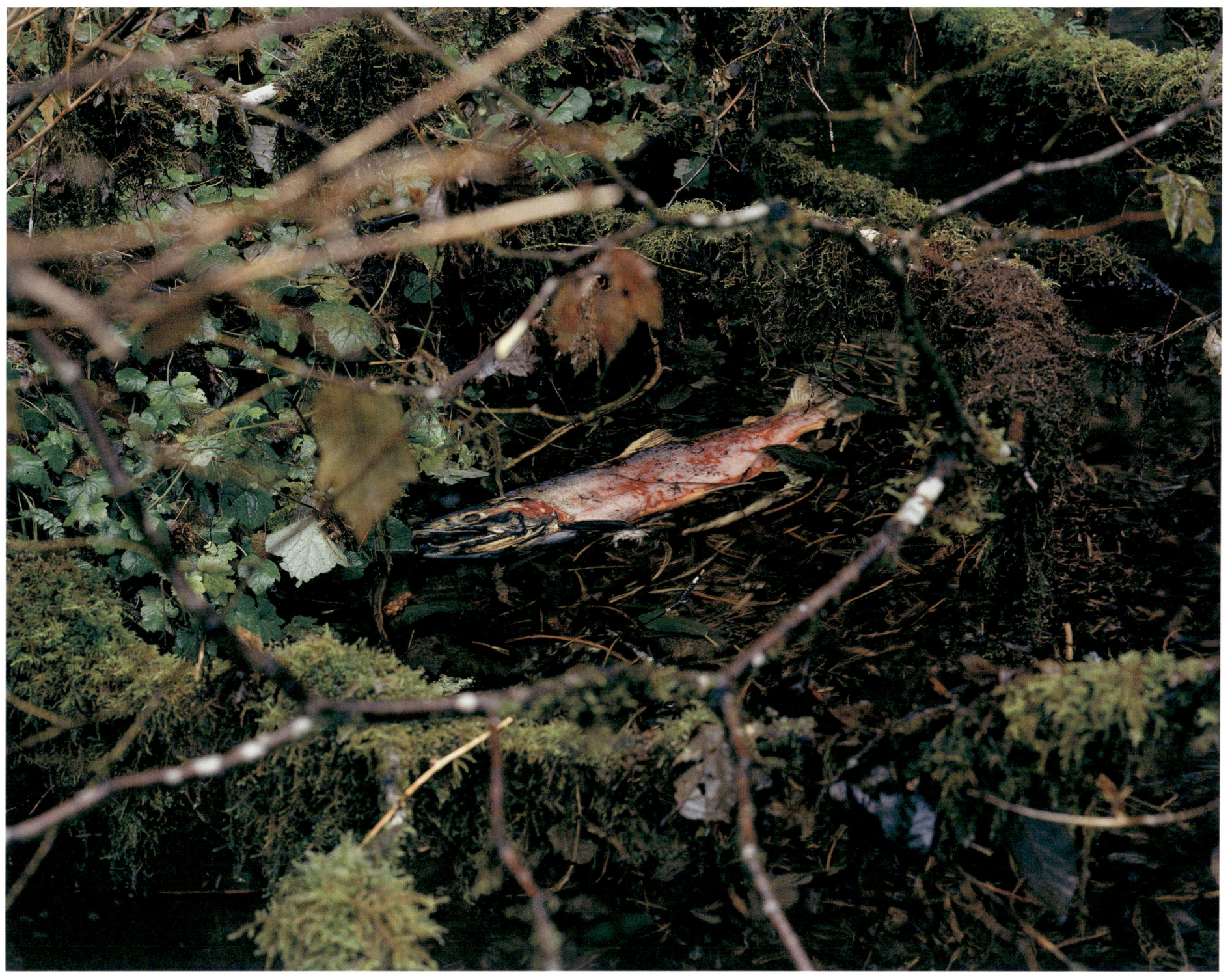

Spawned Coho, upper Sol Duc River, Washington   25

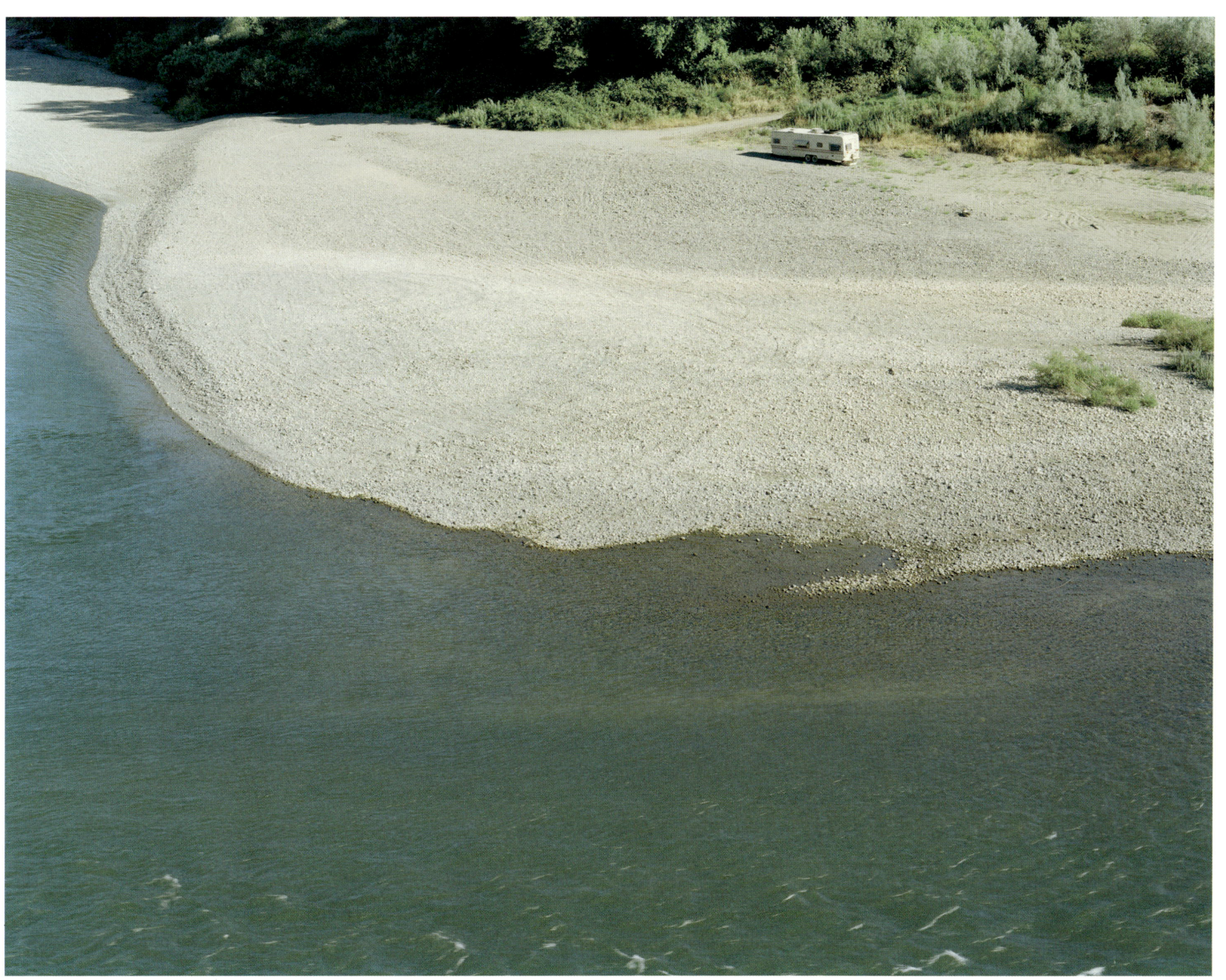

Confluence of the Rogue and Illinois Rivers, Oregon   27

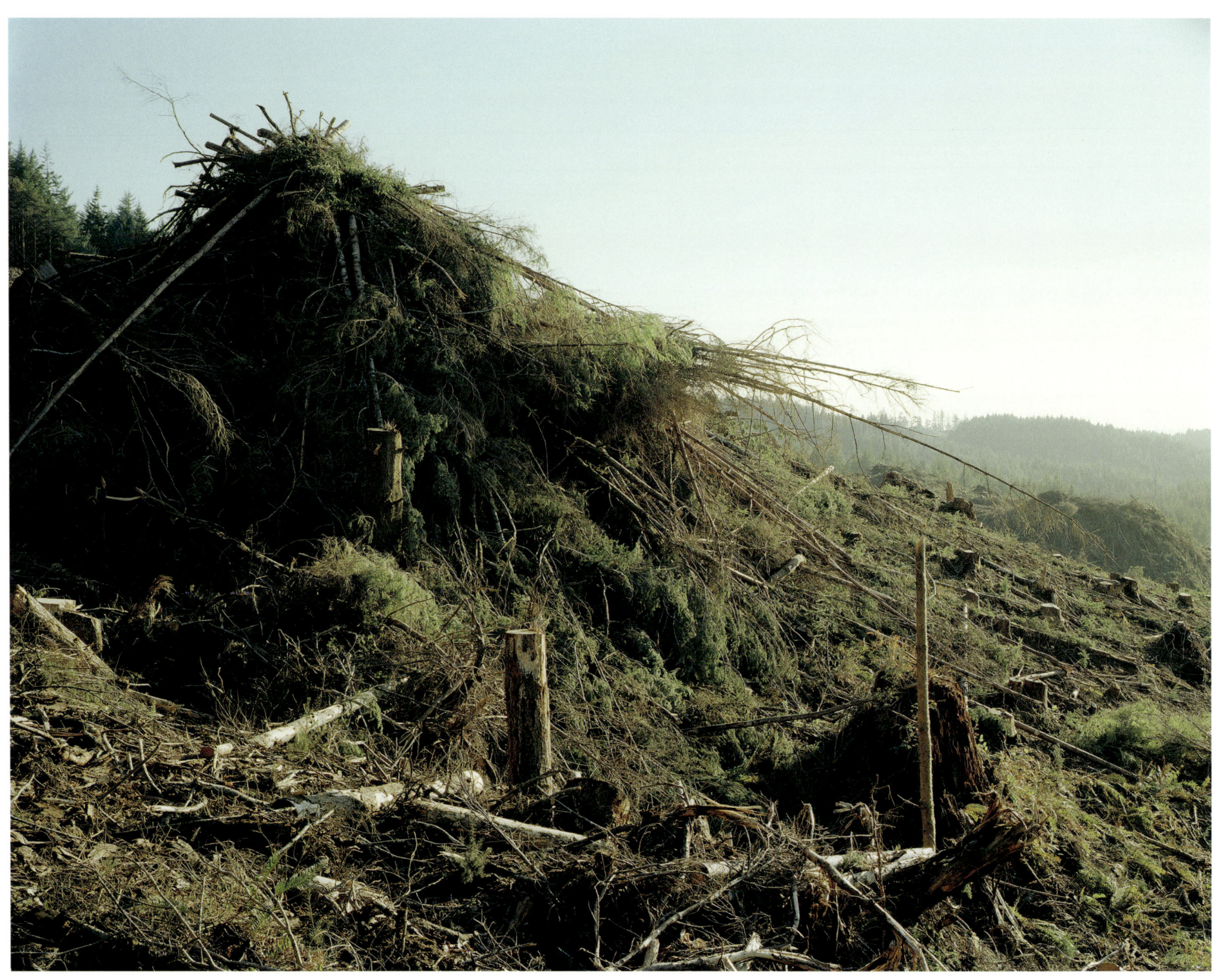

28   Clear-cut burn pile, Oregon

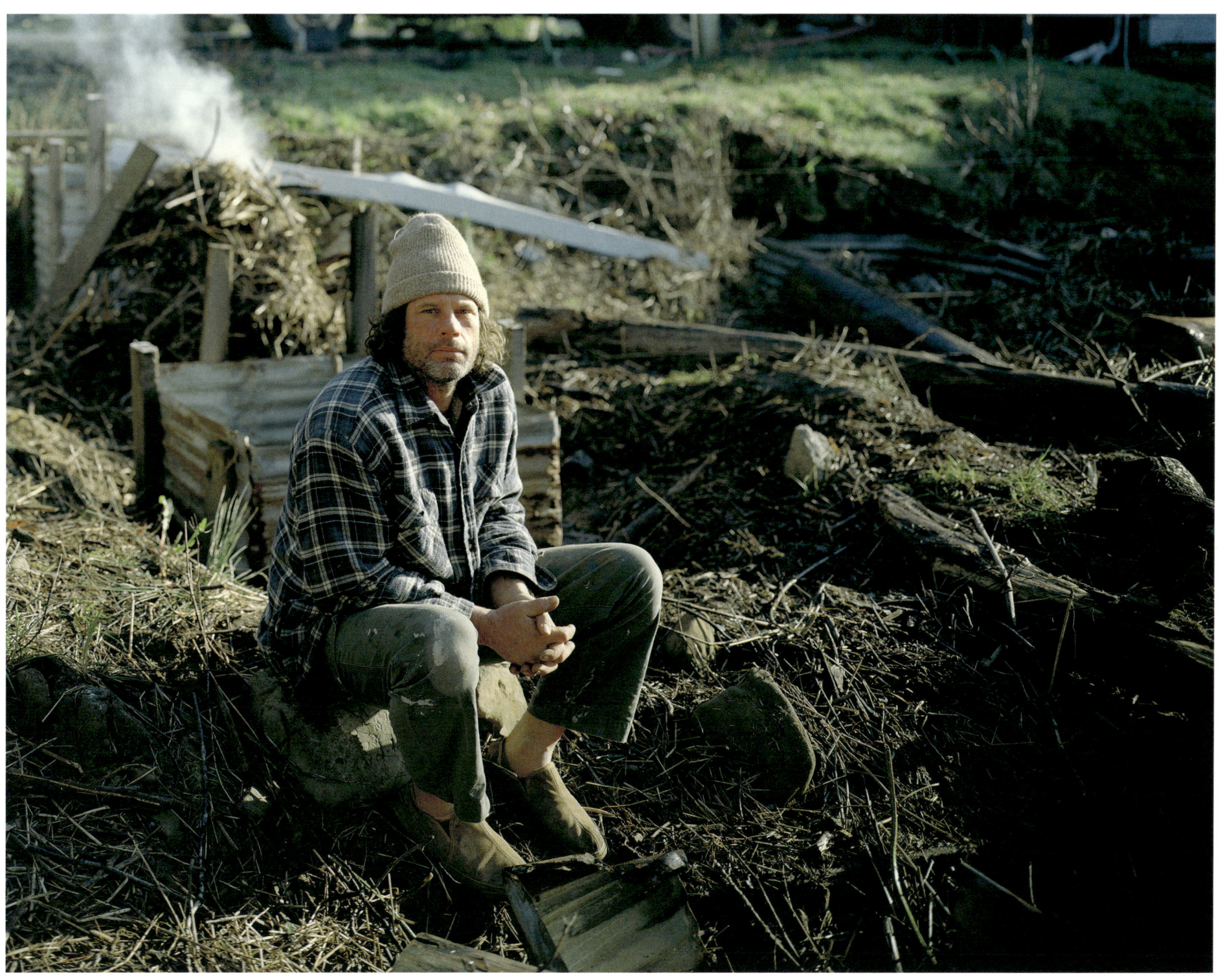

Erin Rieman along the Siuslaw River, Oregon   29

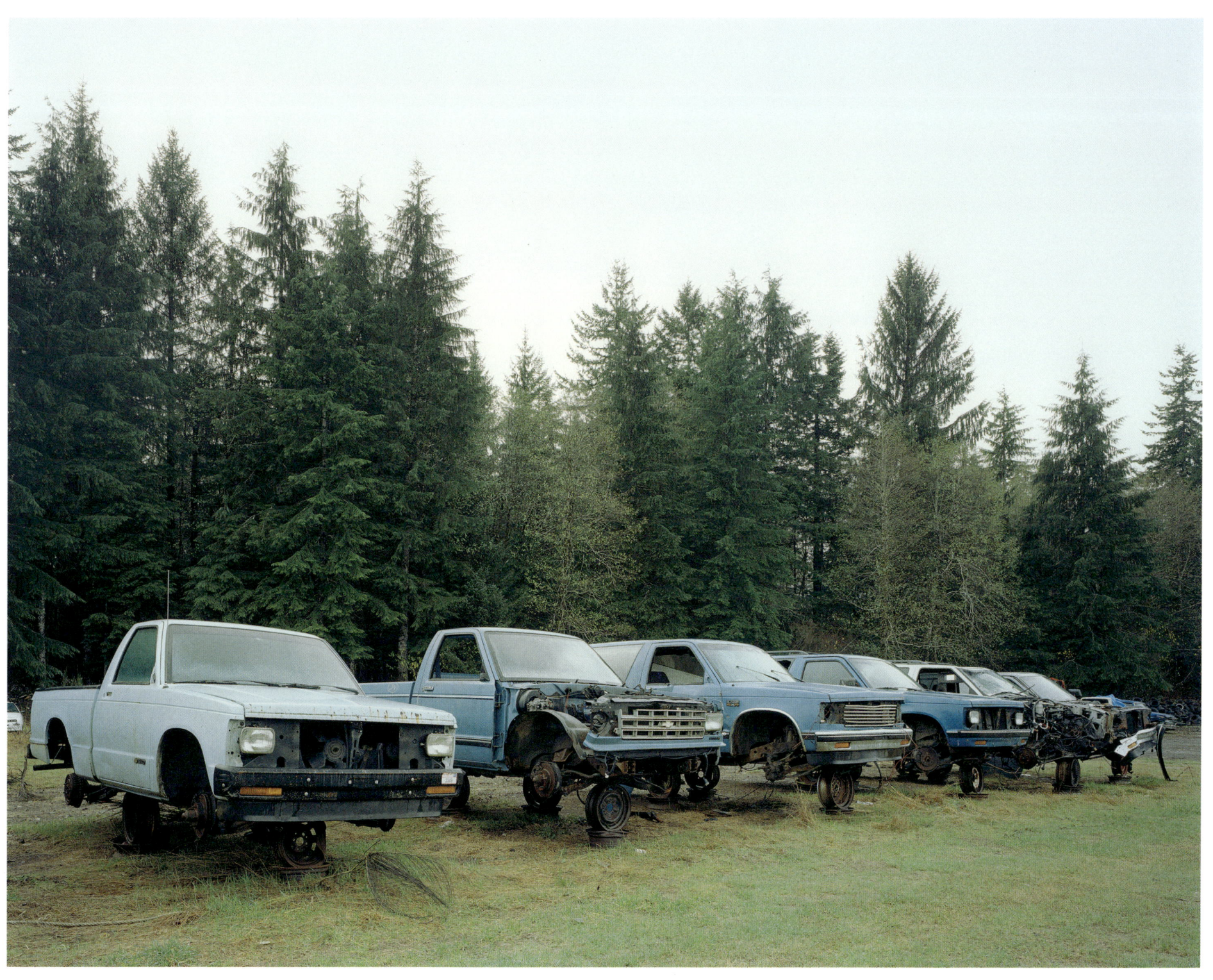

Junked blue trucks, Forks, Washington 31

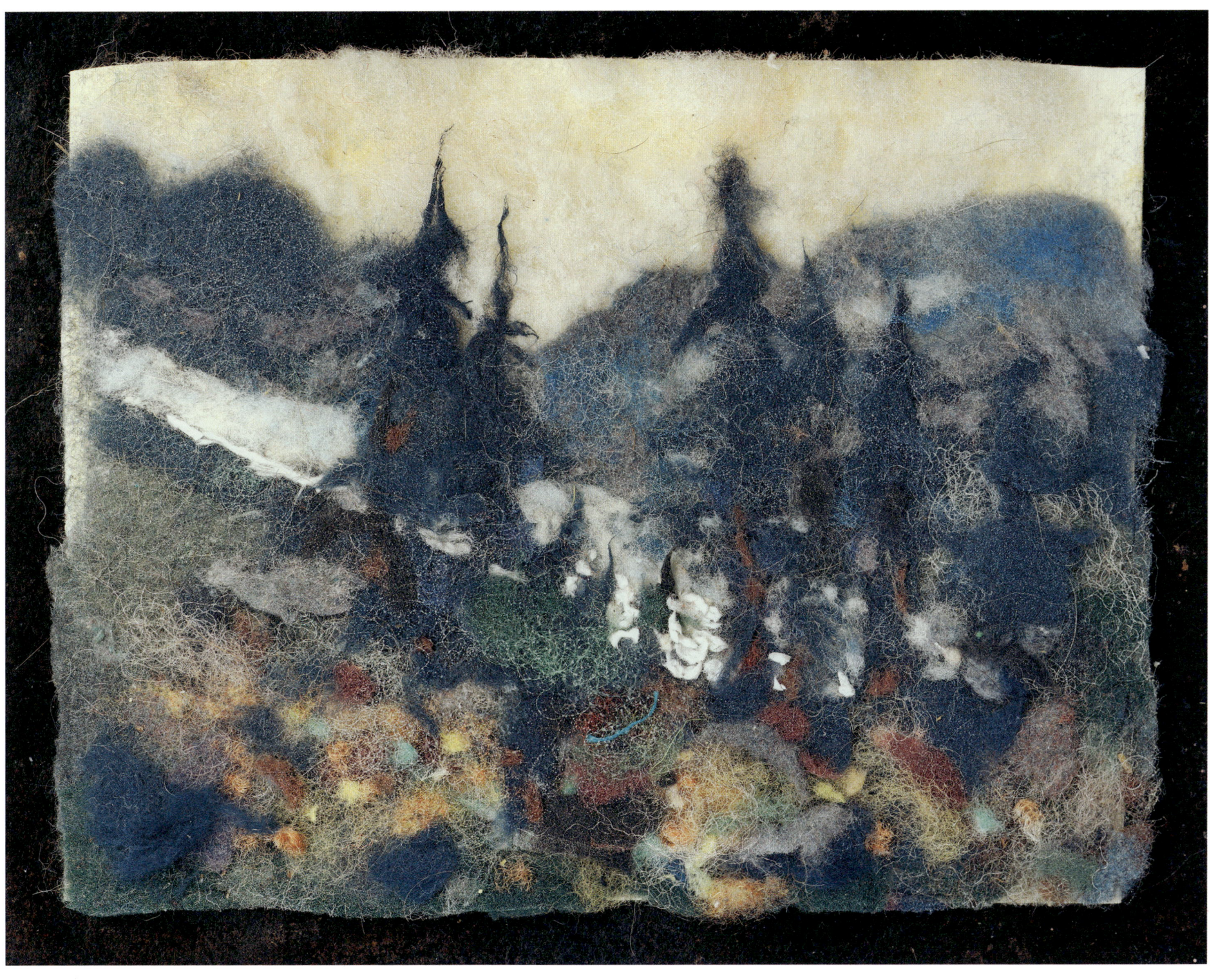

Missy Barlow's dryer lint landscape, lower Hoh River, Washington   33

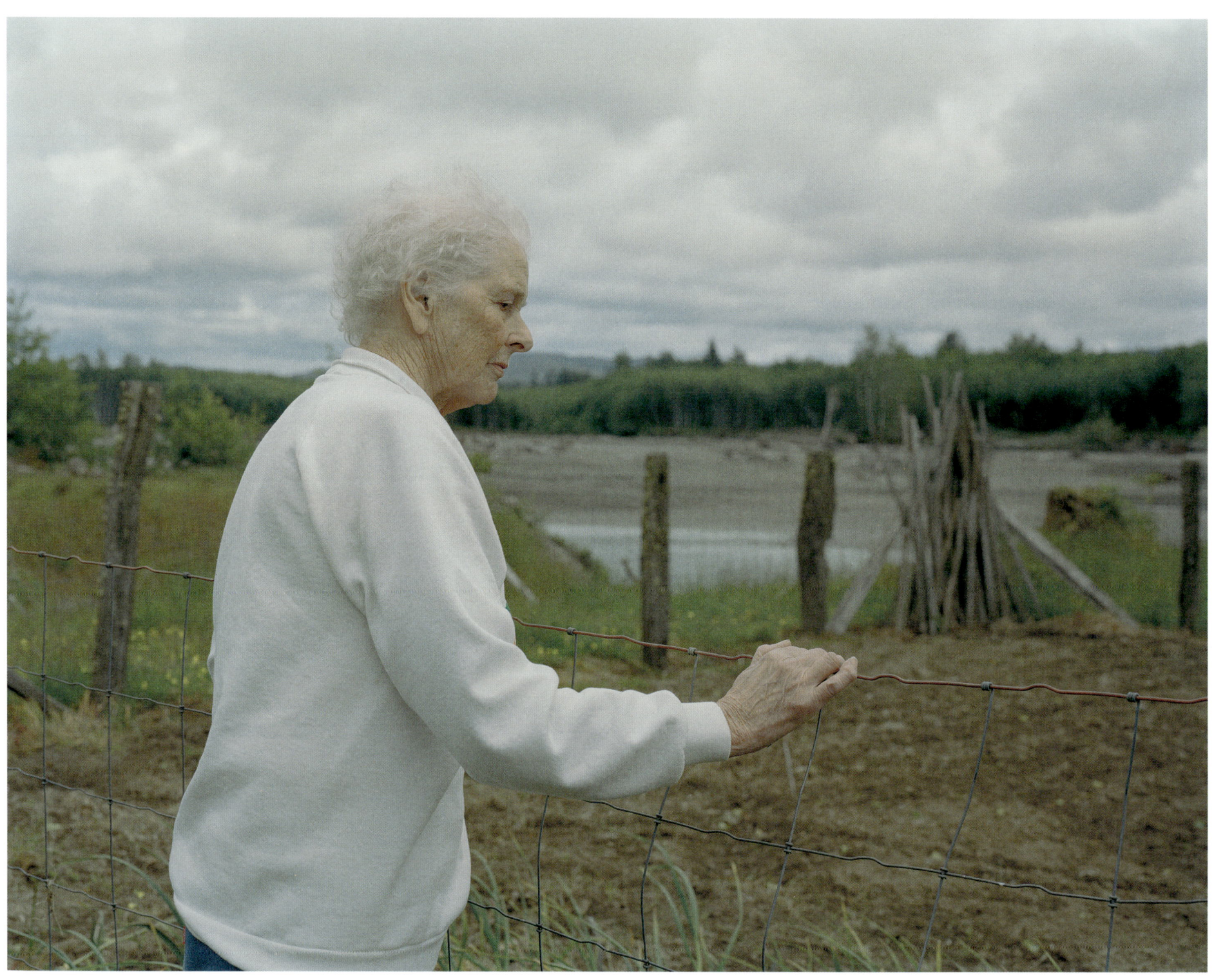

34   Missy by her garden, lower Hoh River, Washington

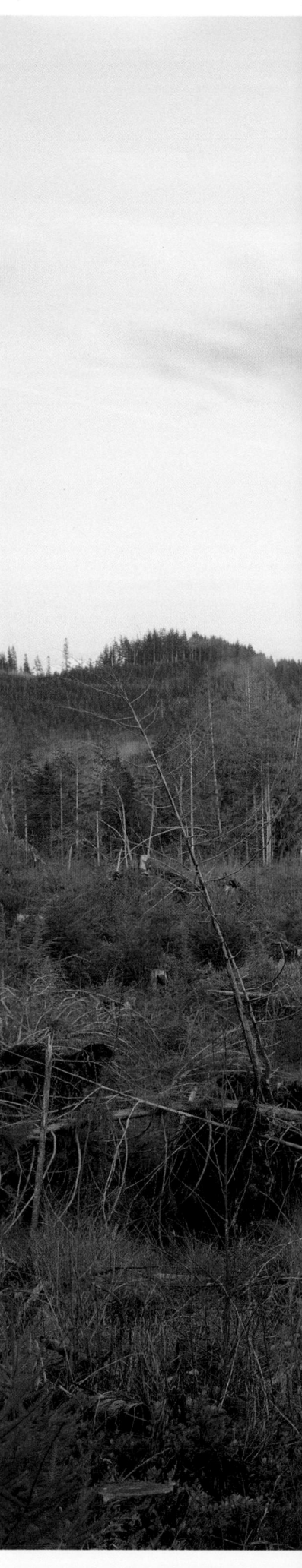

36   Adolescent bald eagle, Queets, Washington

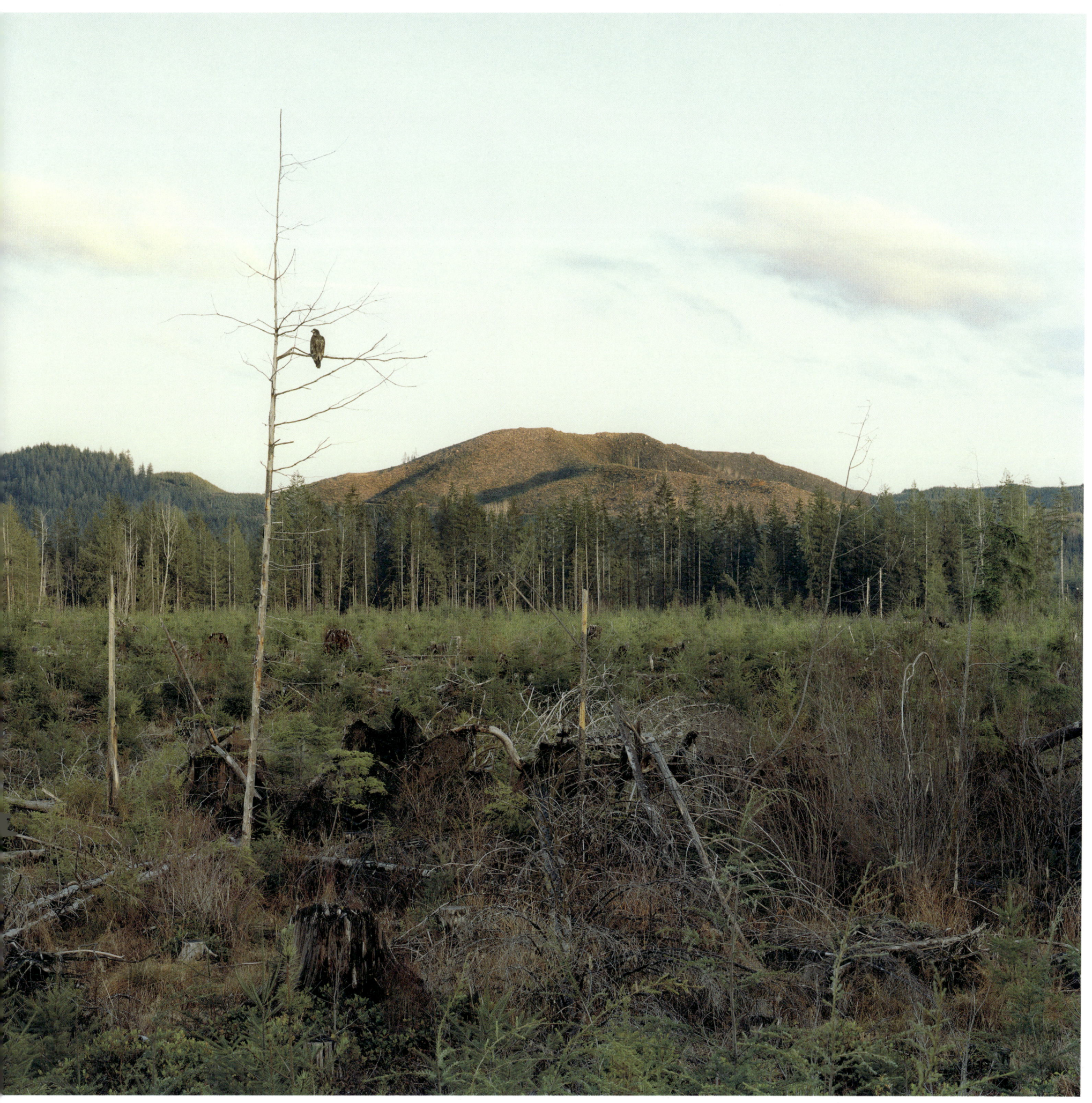

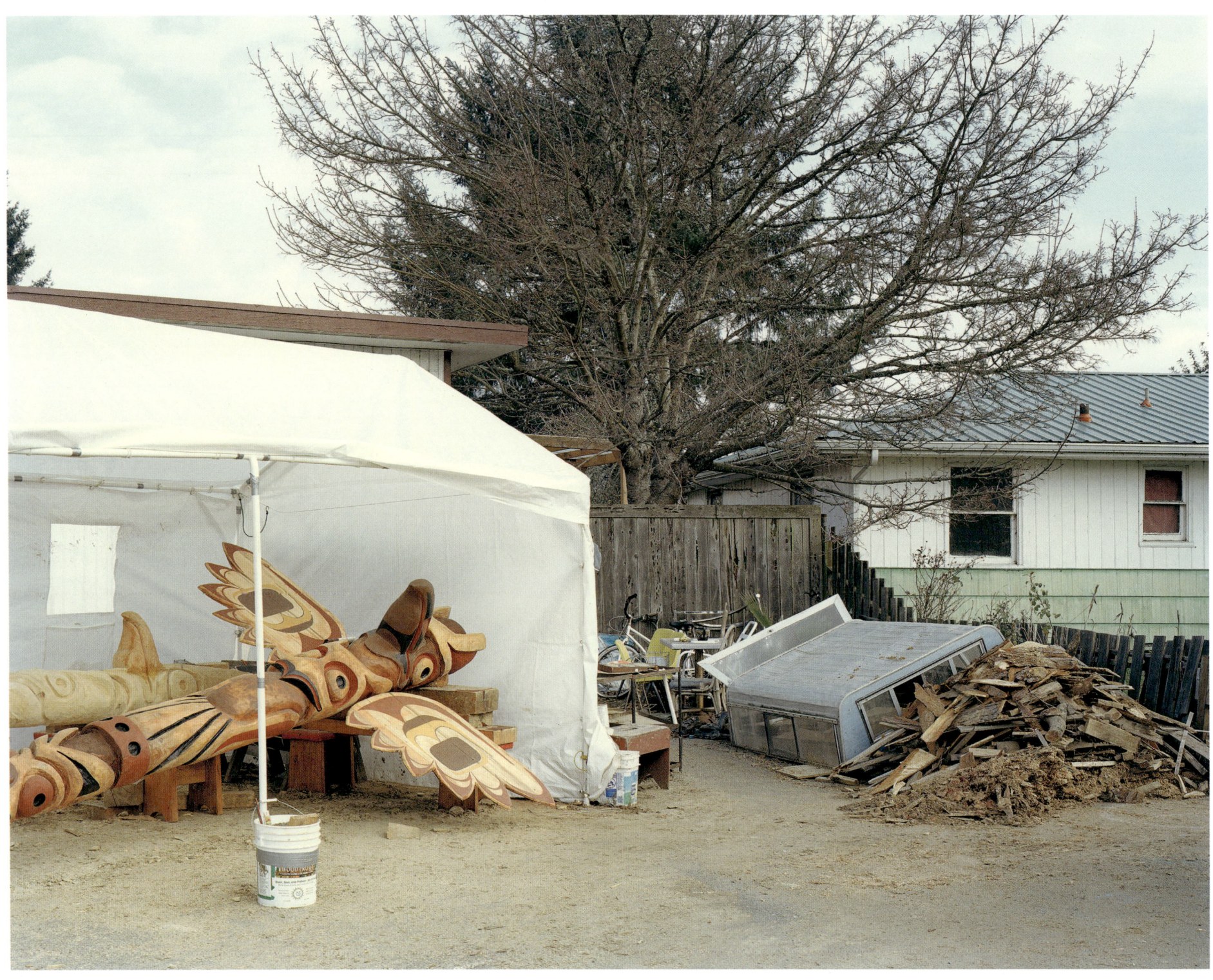

38   Totem poles, Winston, Oregon

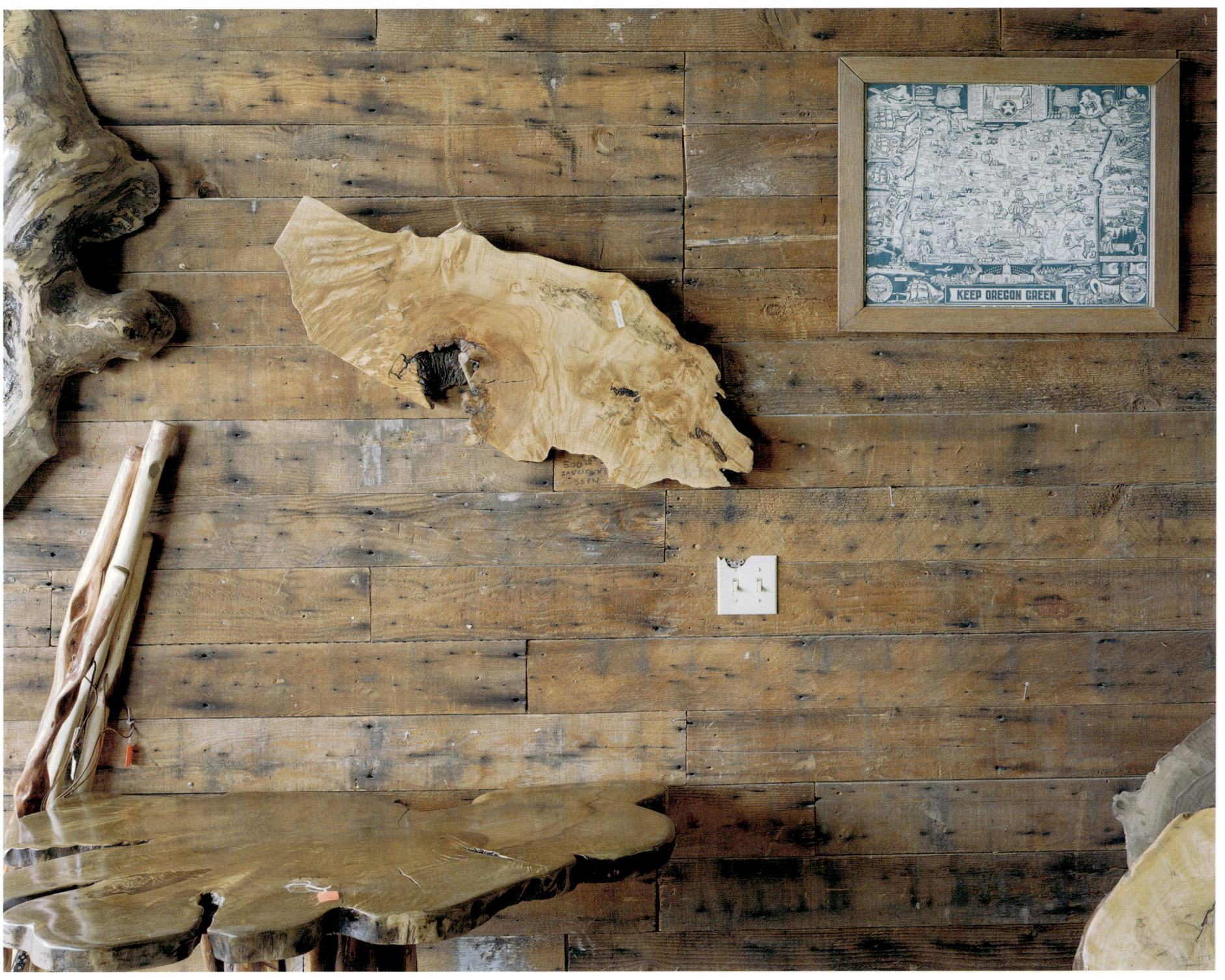

Art of Wood store, North Bend, Oregon   39

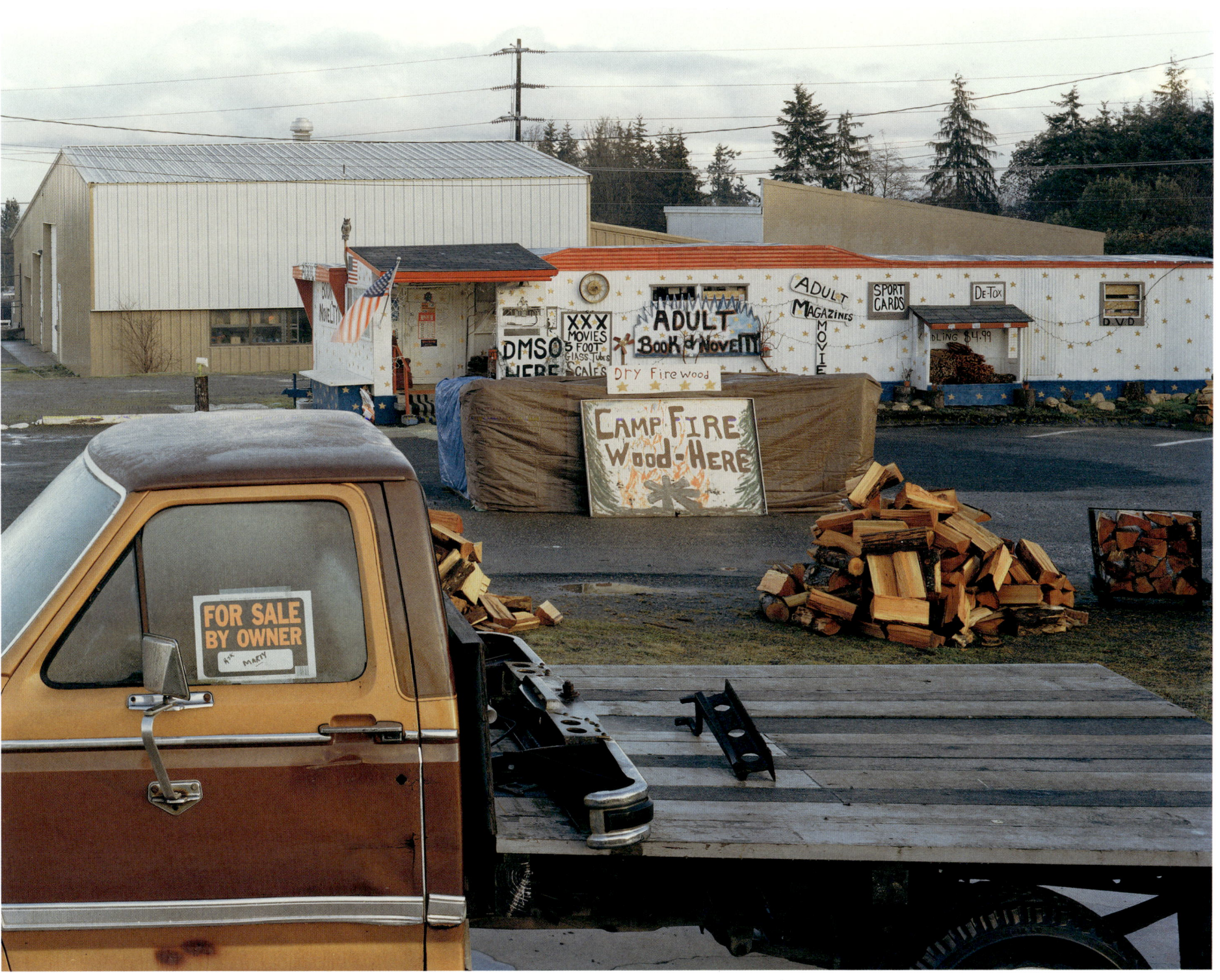

Adult books, firewood, and truck for sale, Port Angeles, Washington   41

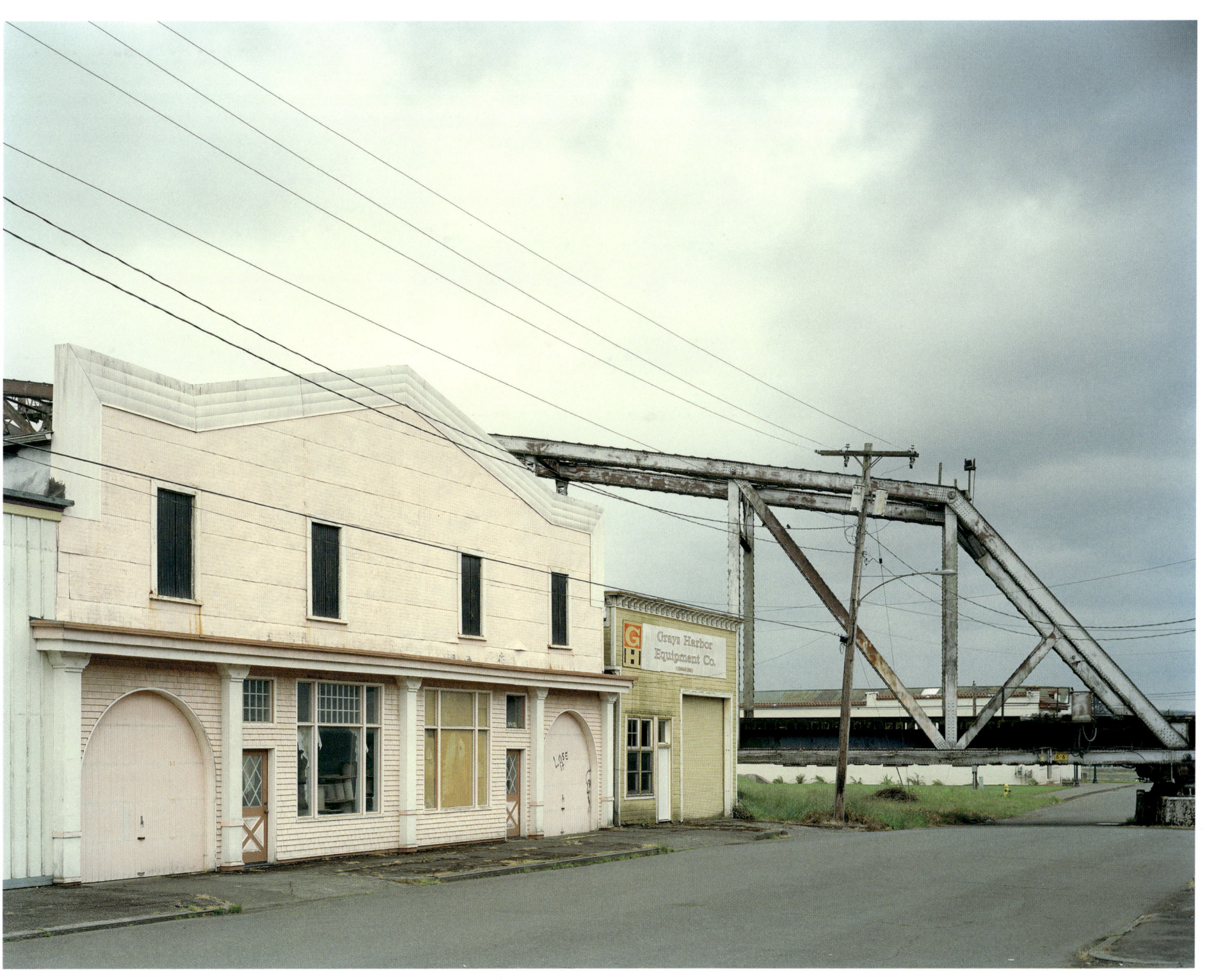

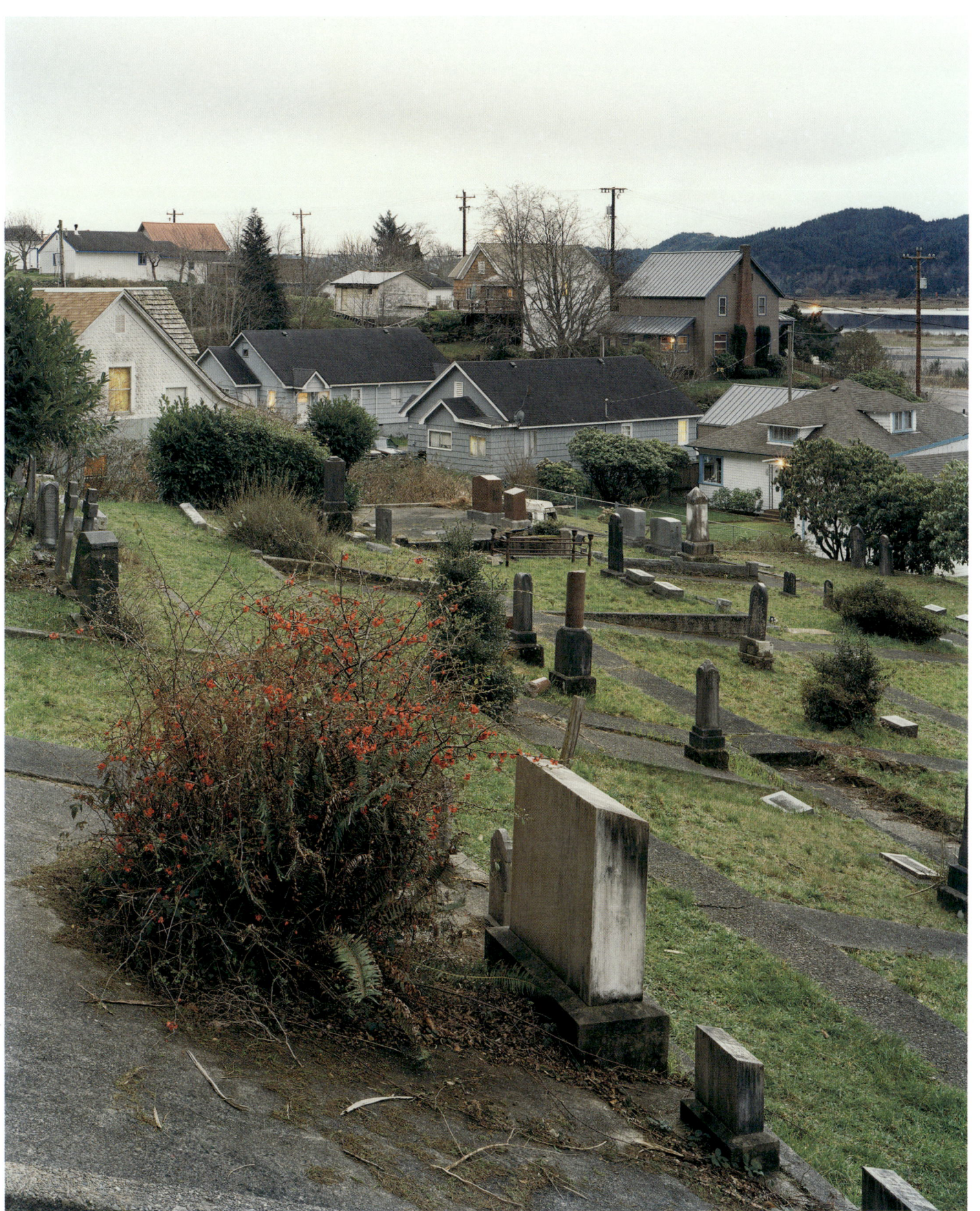

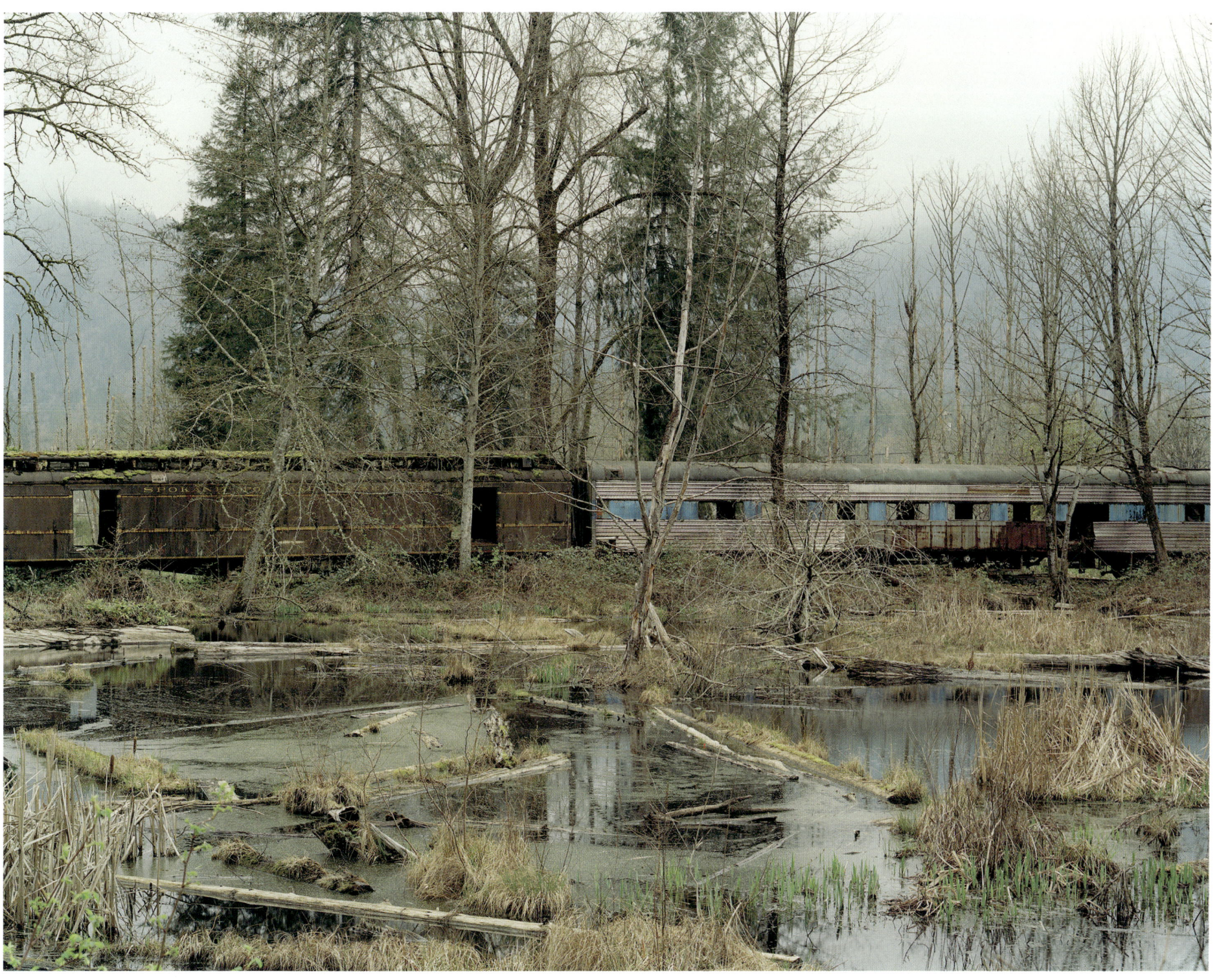

Scrapped train, Arlington, Washington   47

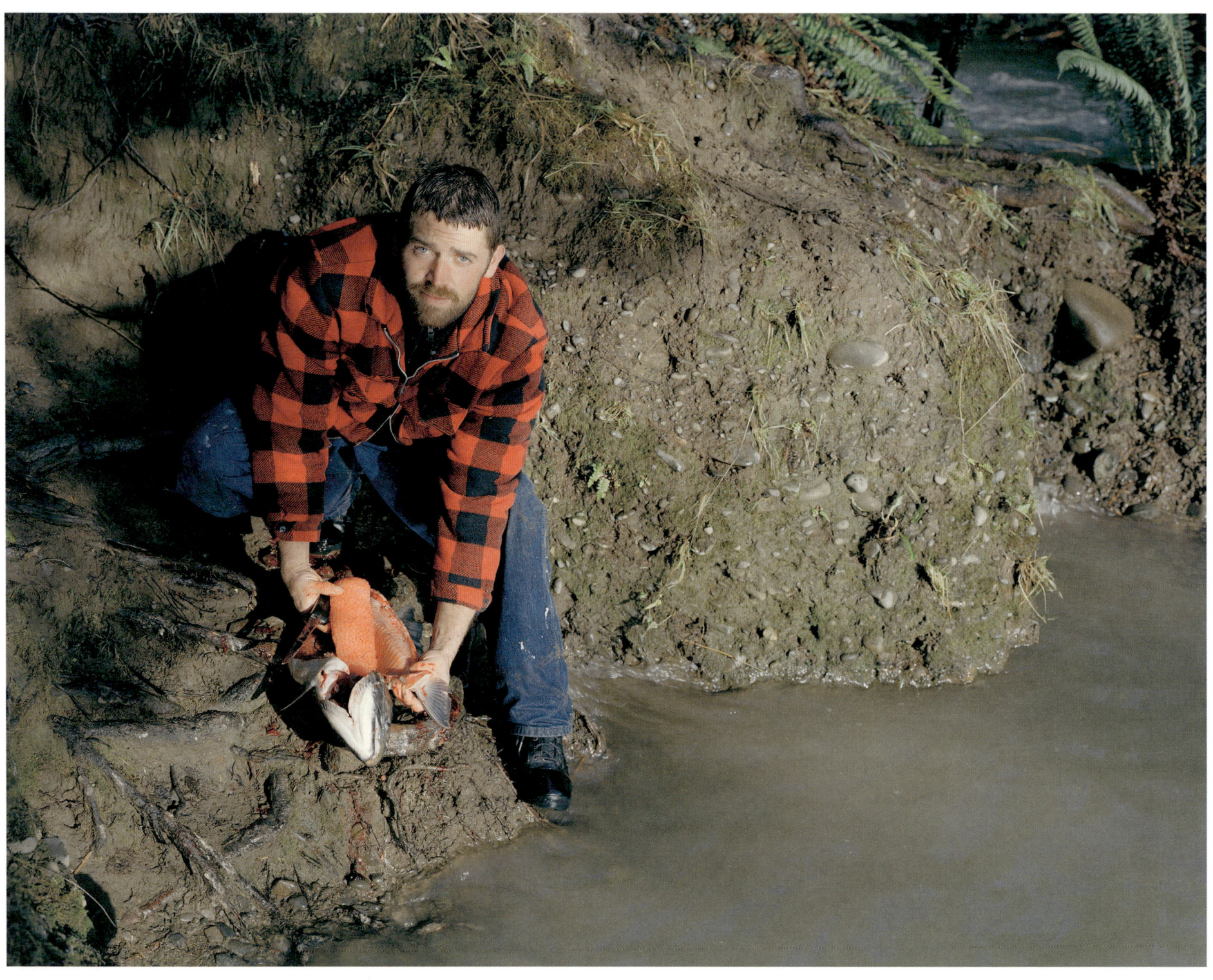

48   Josh cleaning a Chinook along the Sol Duc River, Washington

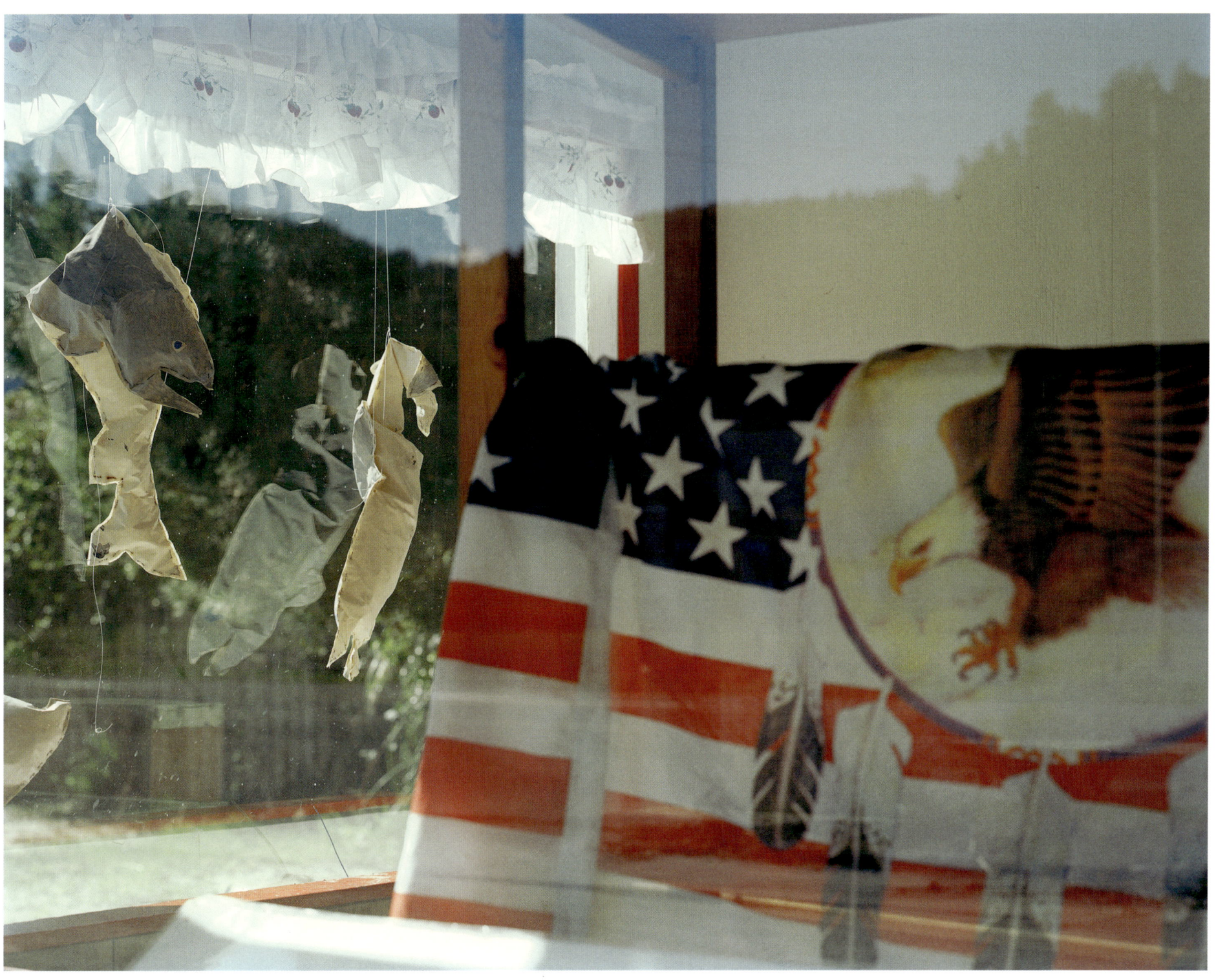

Salmon jerky stand, Hoppaw, California   49

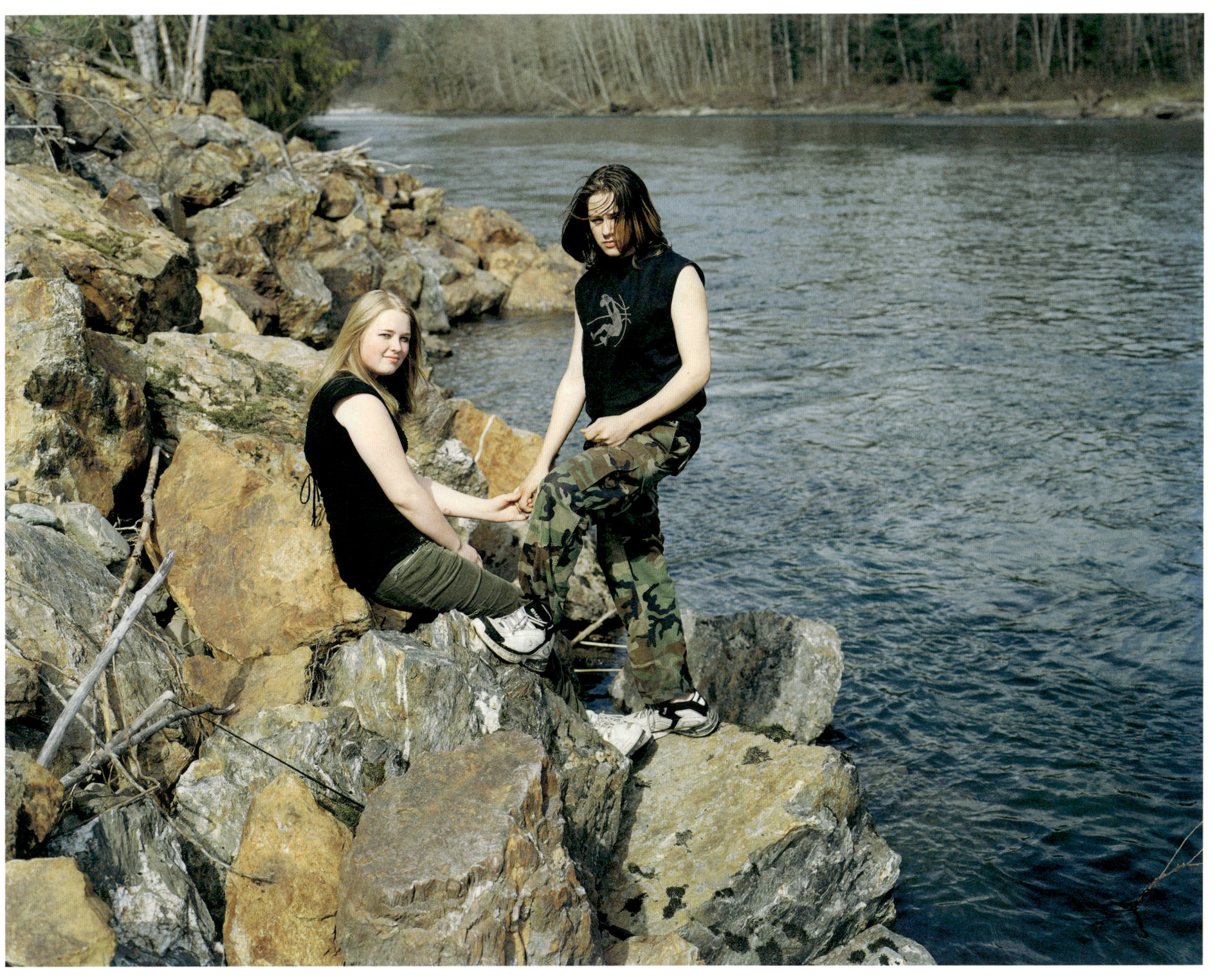

Deborah and William along the Sauk River, Washington　51

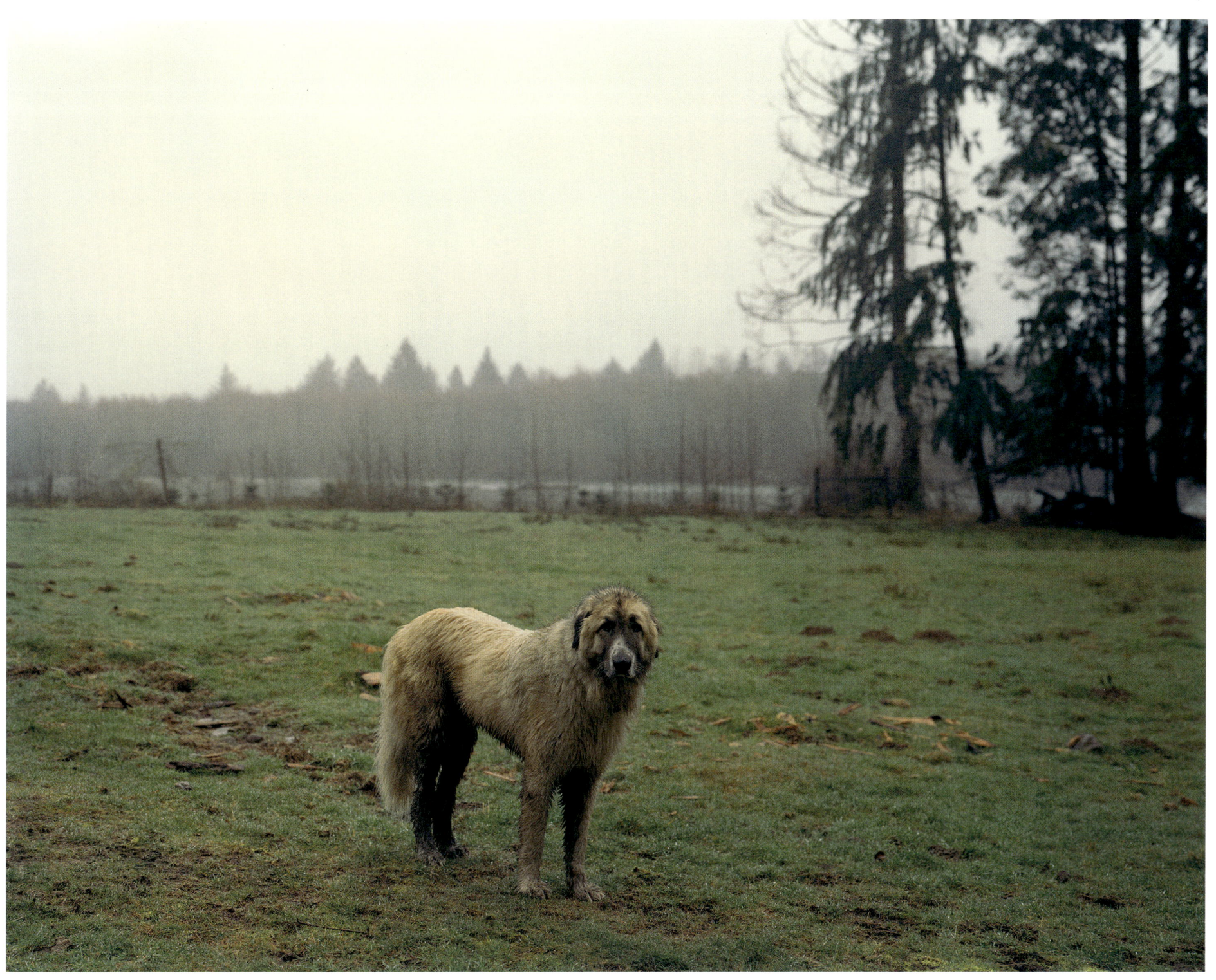

Tola, lower Hoh River, Washington   53

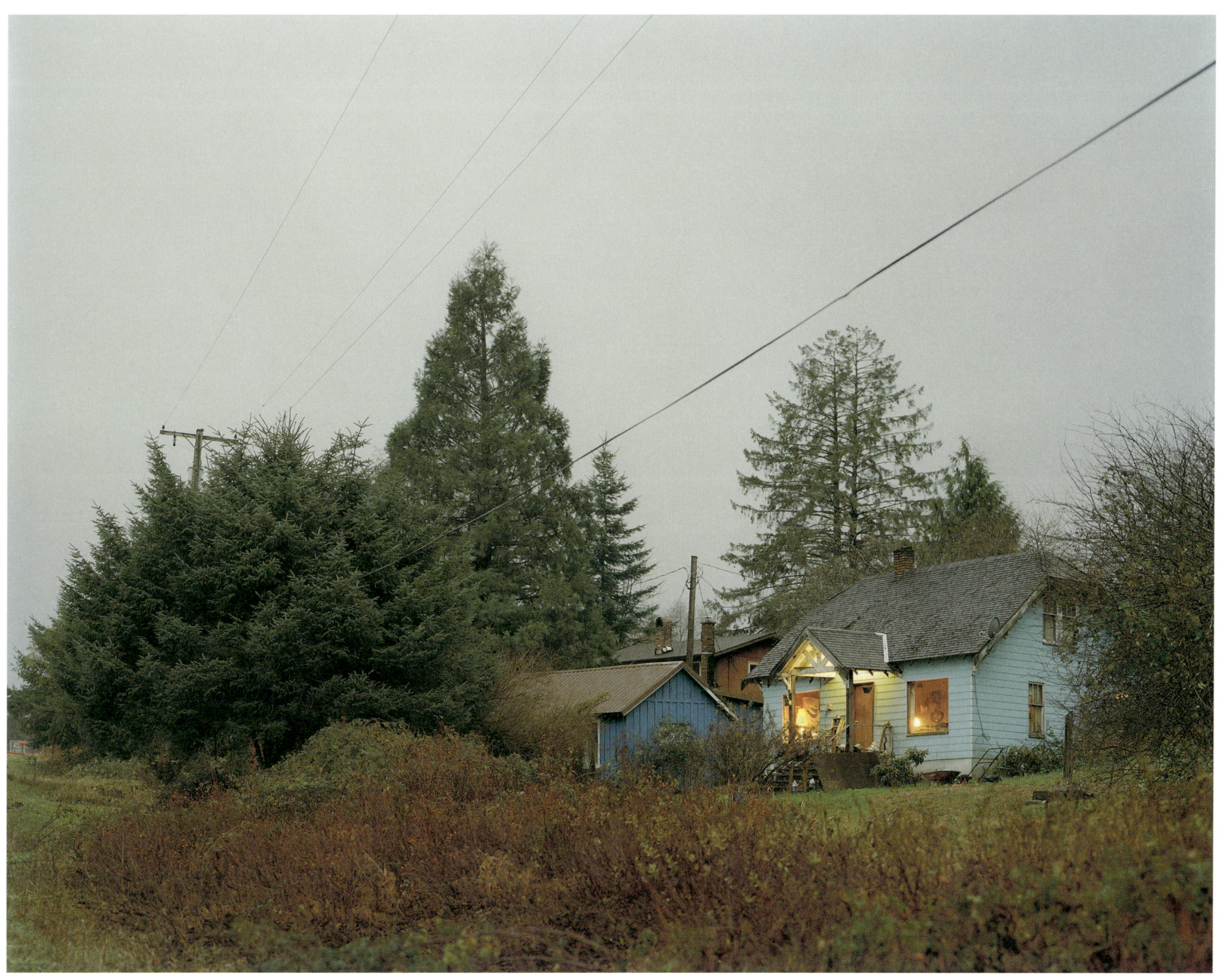

The road to Forks, Washington   55

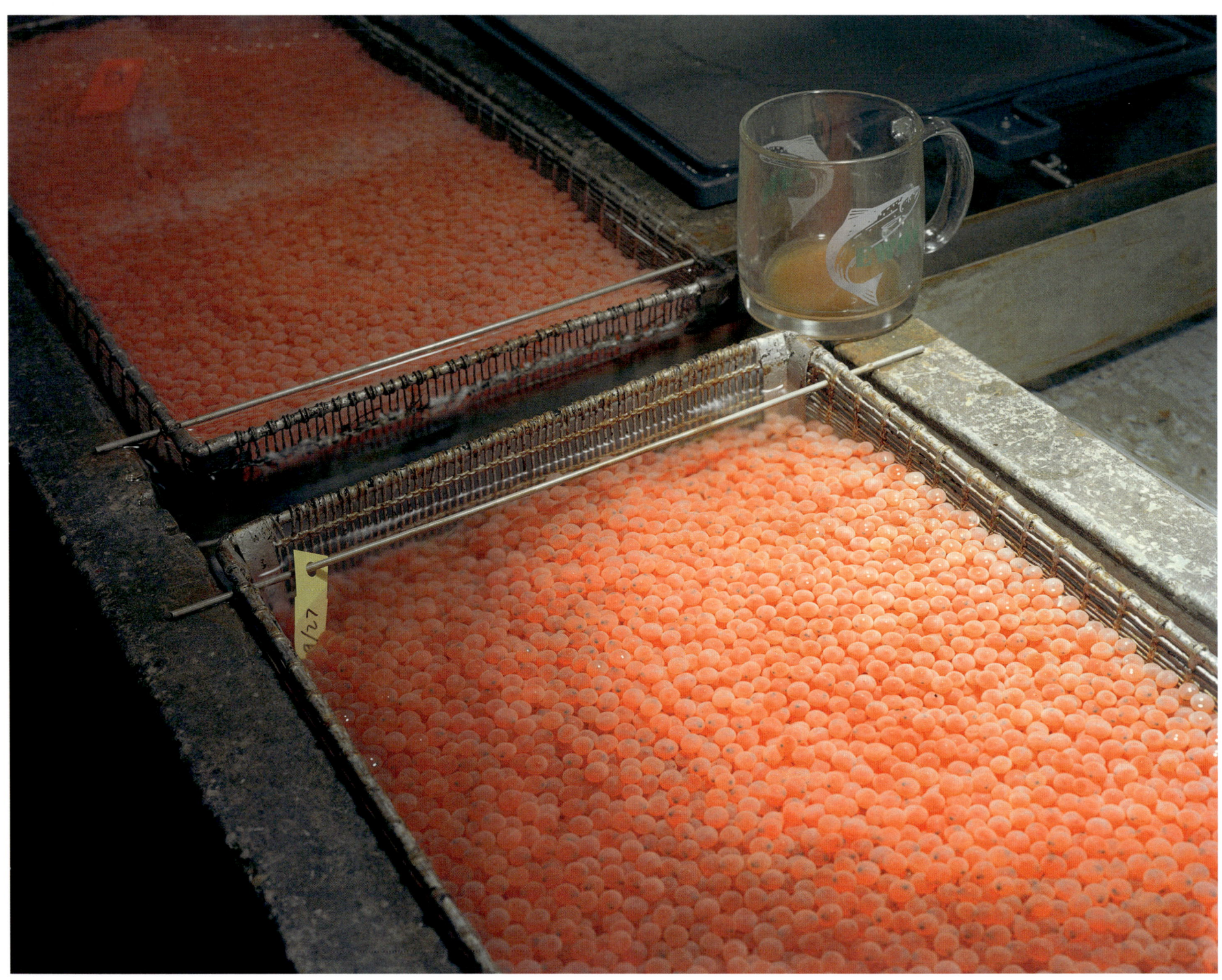

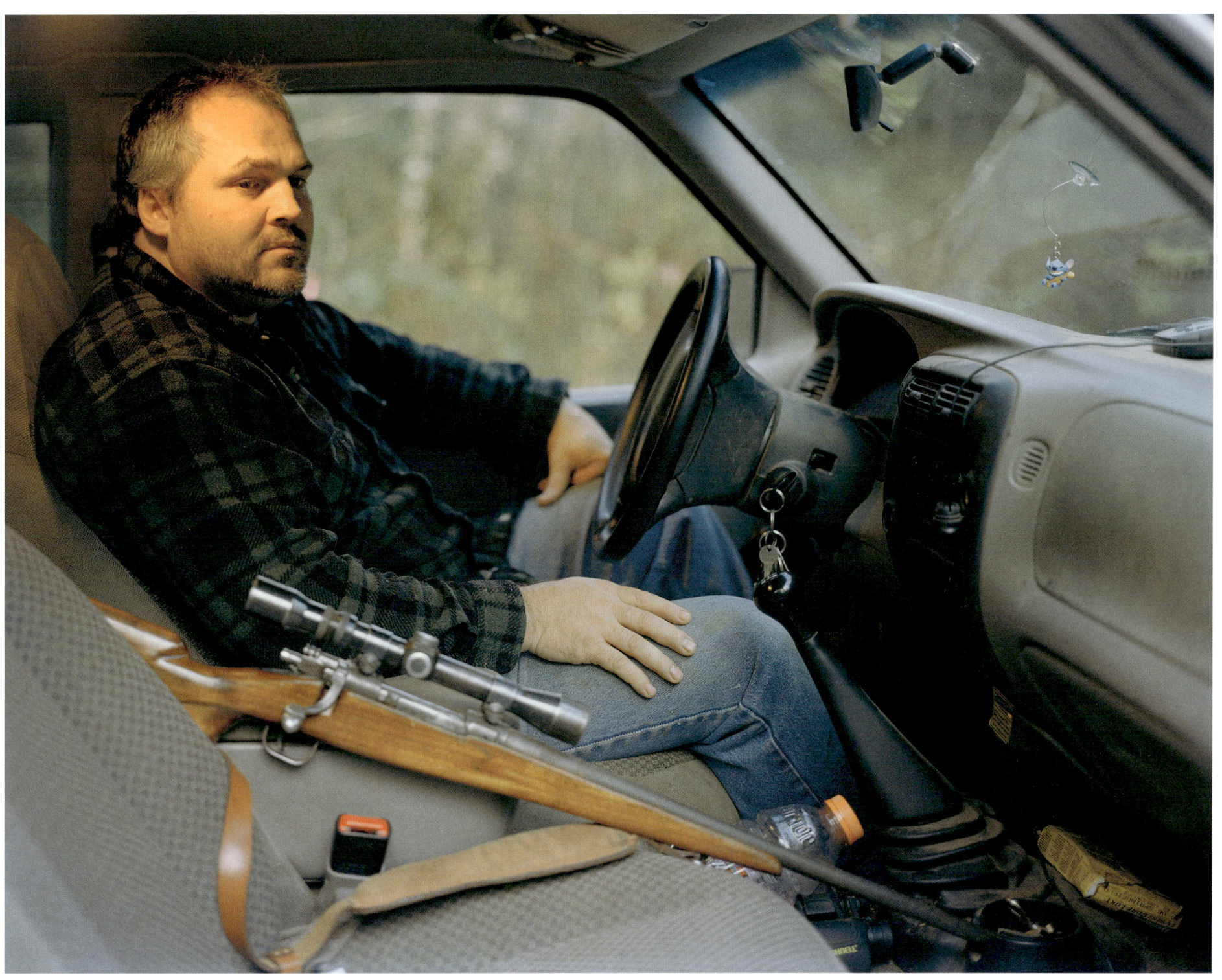

Carl, near Sappho, Washington 57

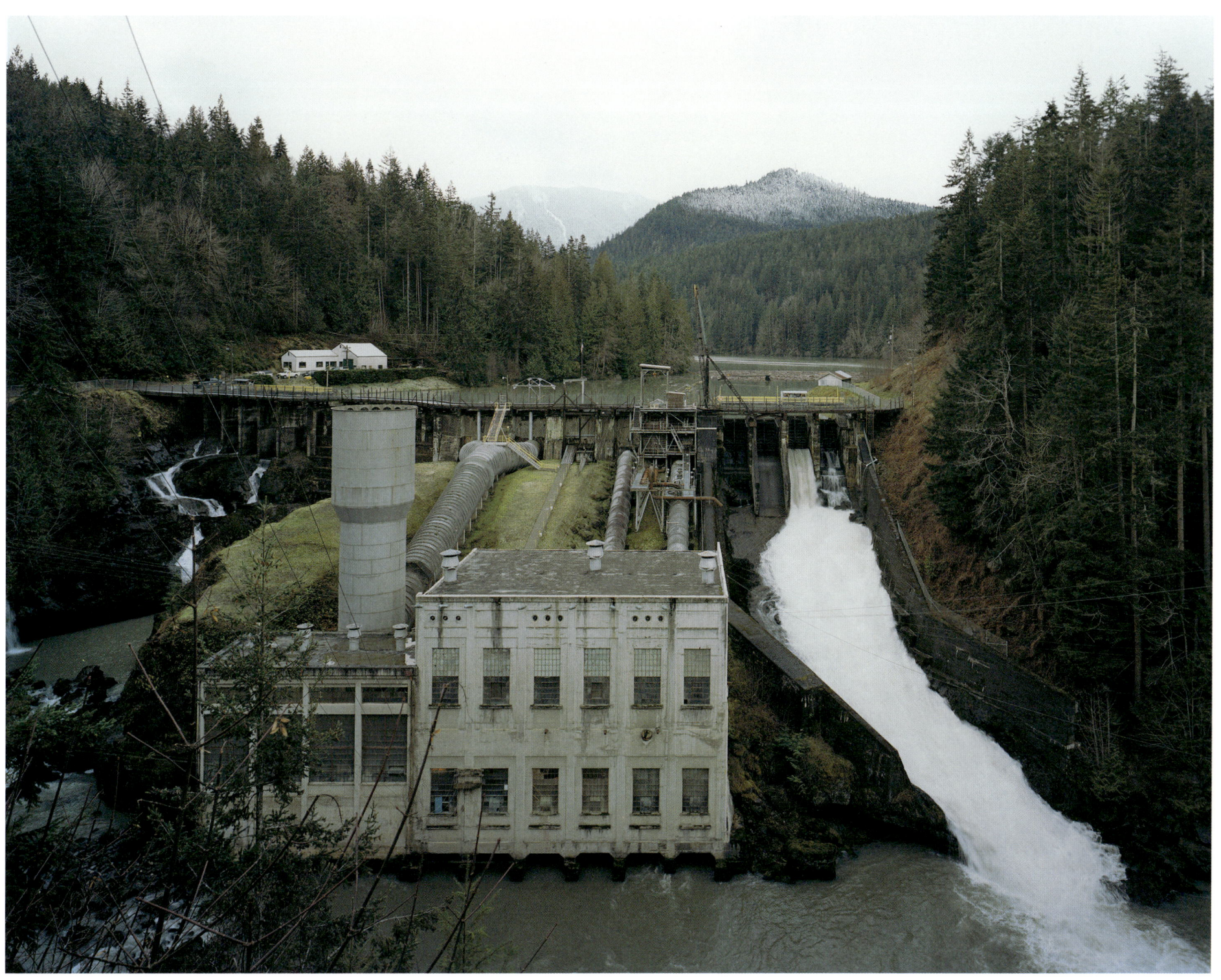

Elwha River Dam, Washington   59

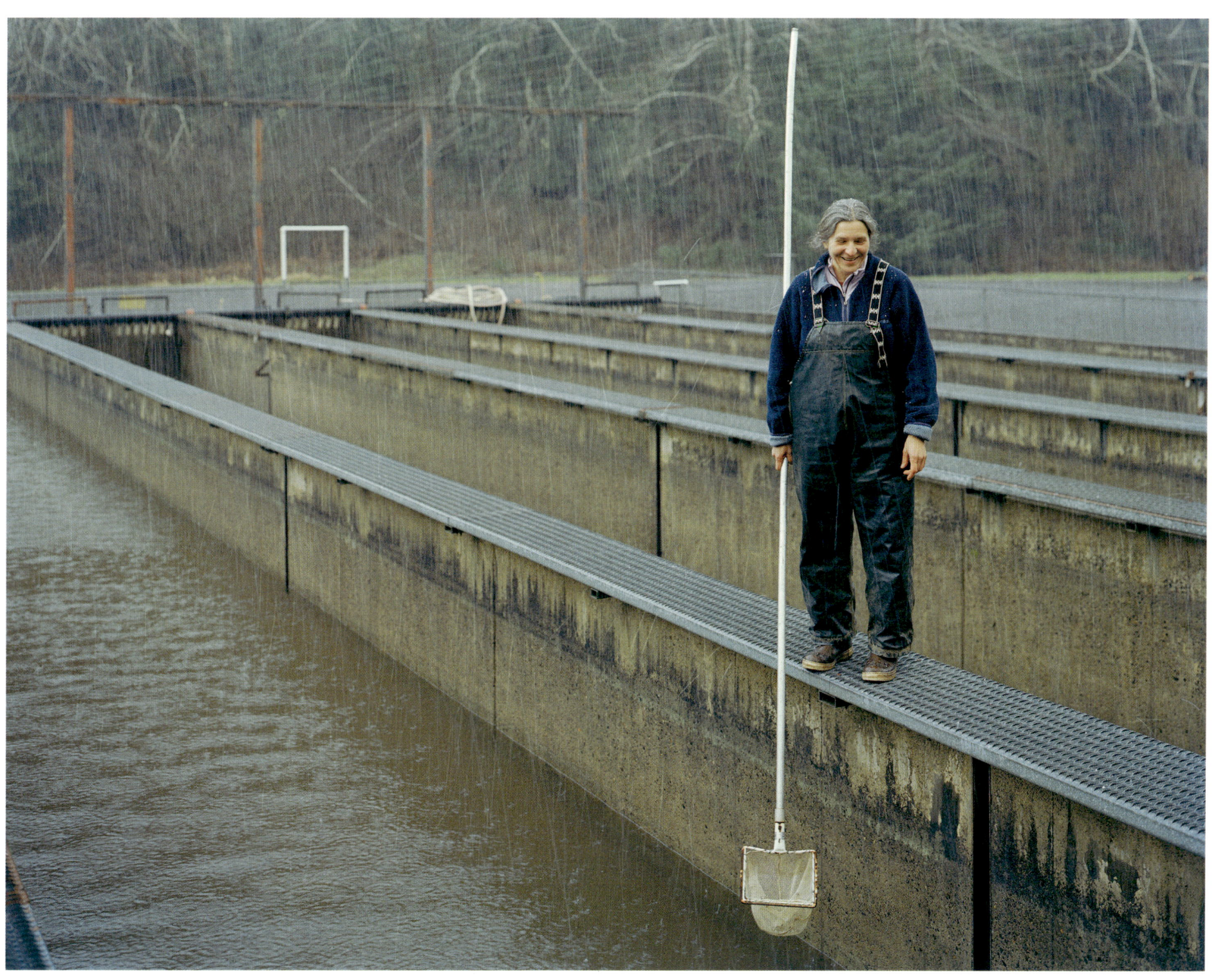

Quinalt tribal gill nets, Queets River, Washington

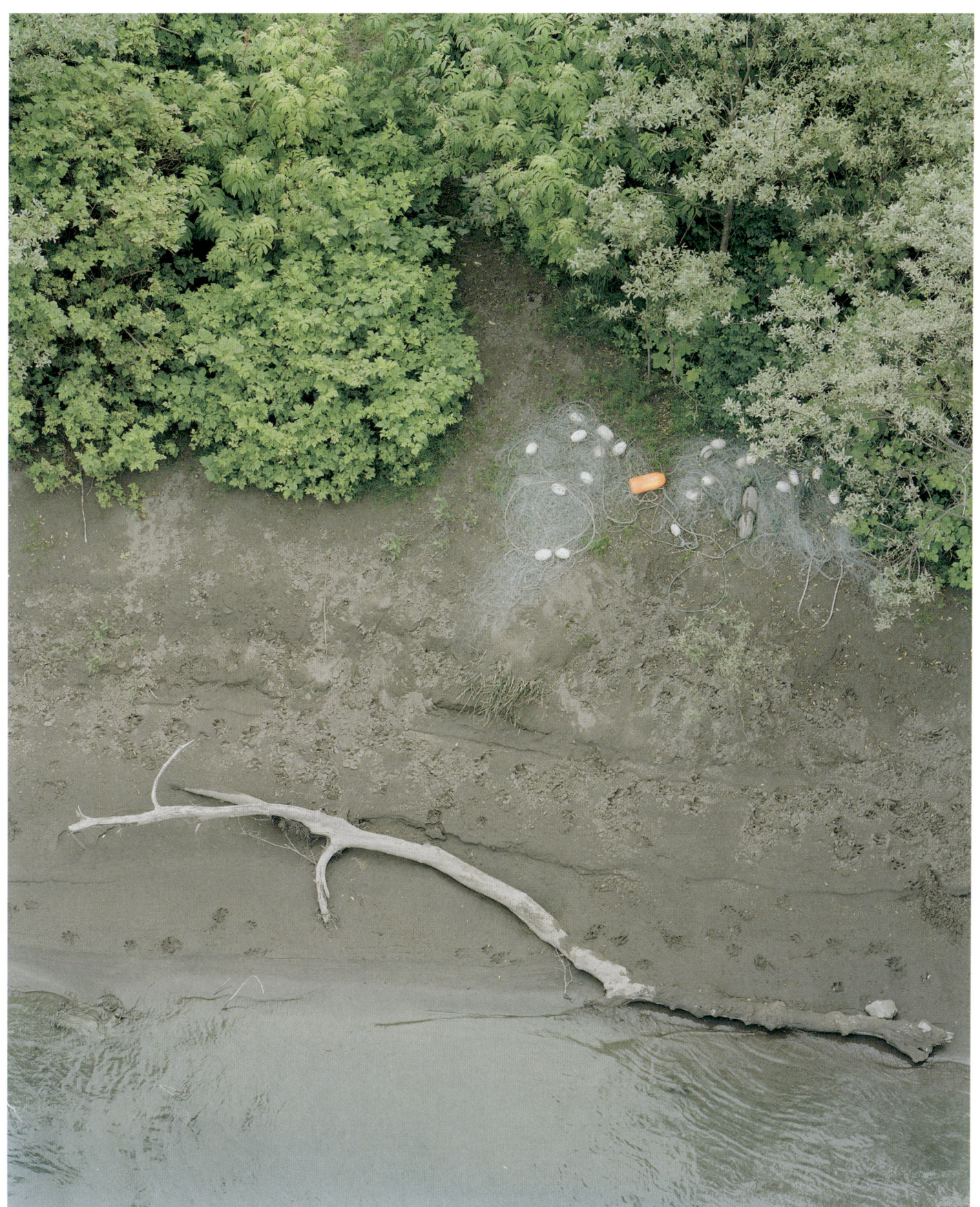

Below the Glines Canyon Dam on the upper Elwha River, Washington

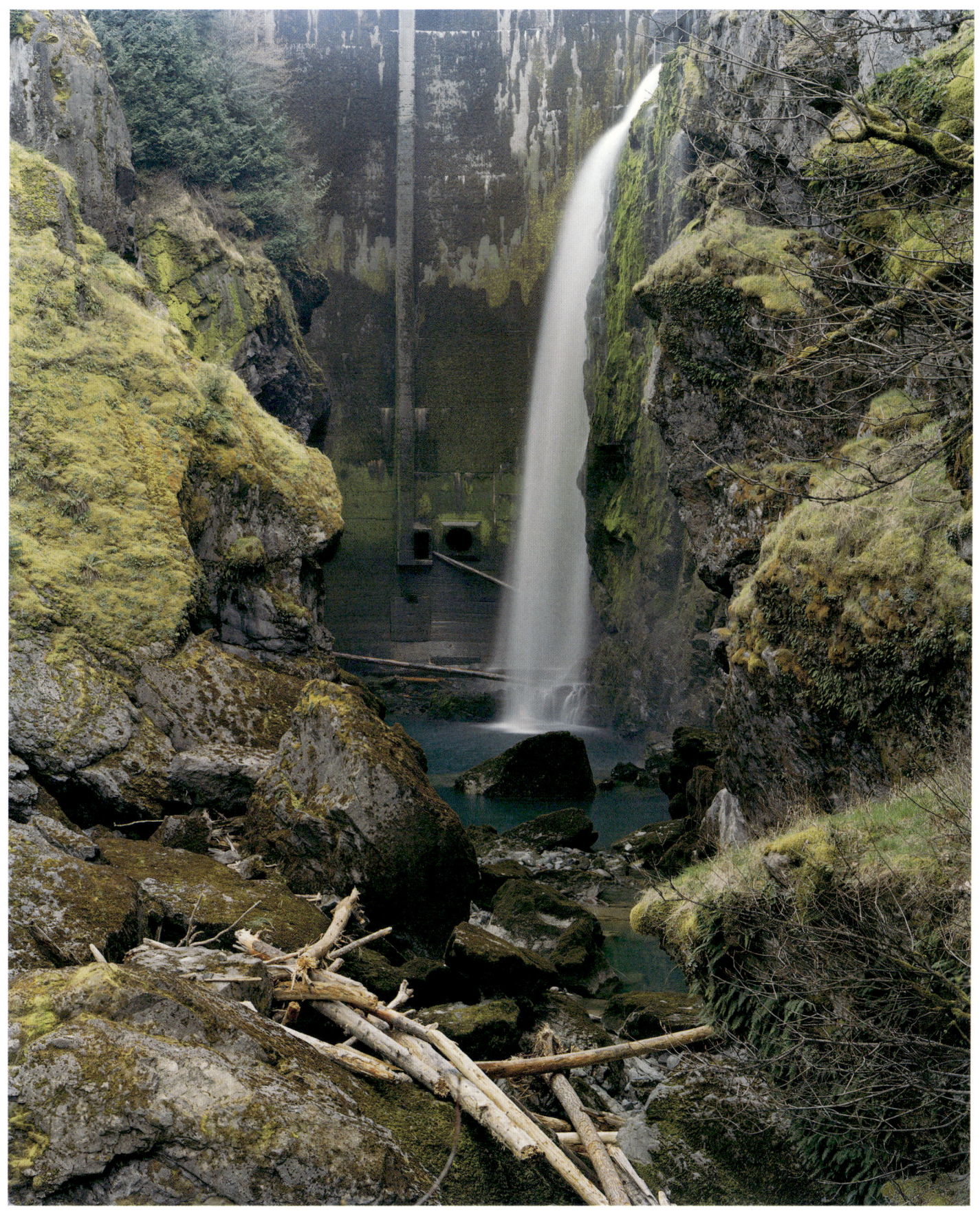

66   Missy, beneath her six-hundred-year-old spruce, Hoh River, Washington

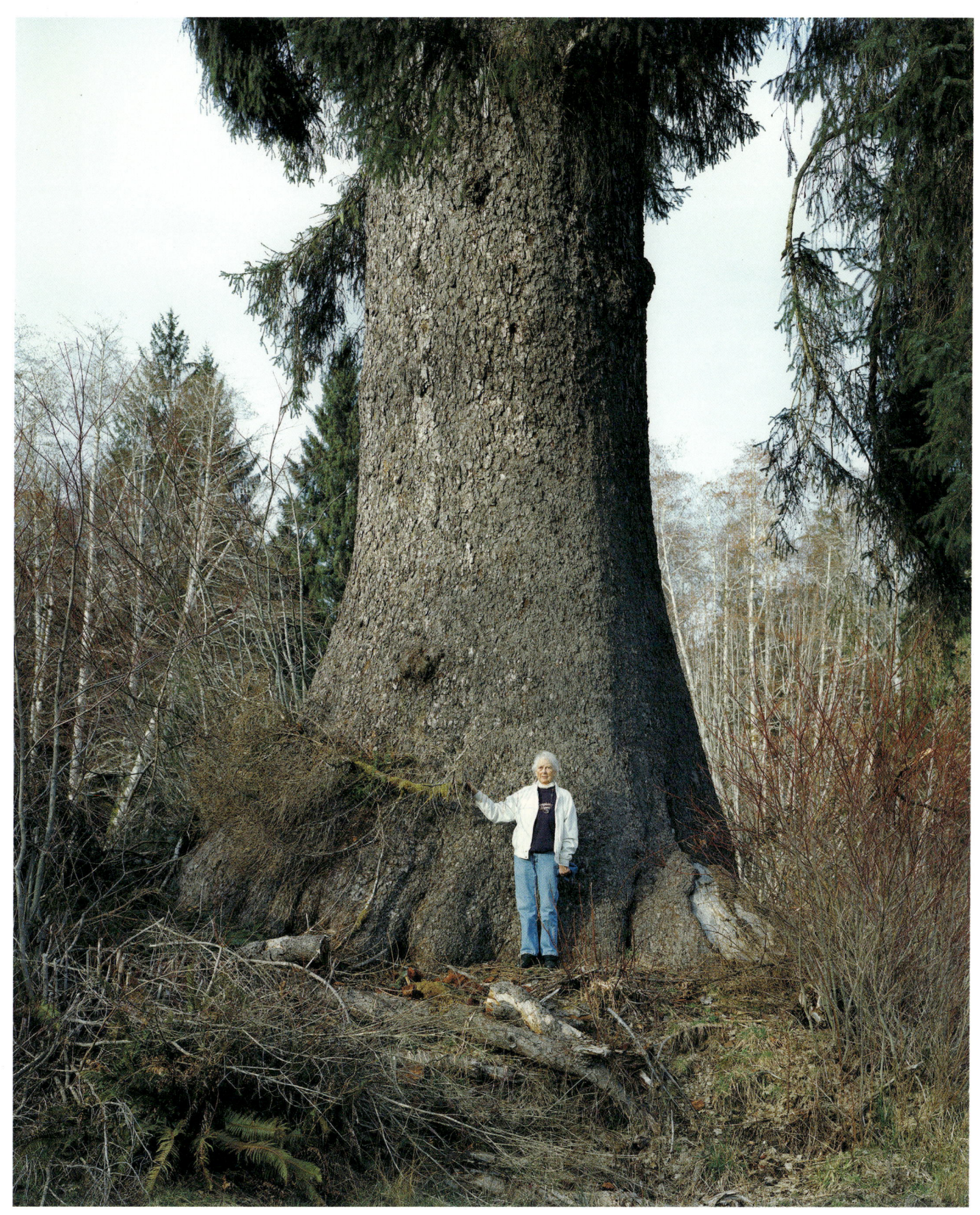

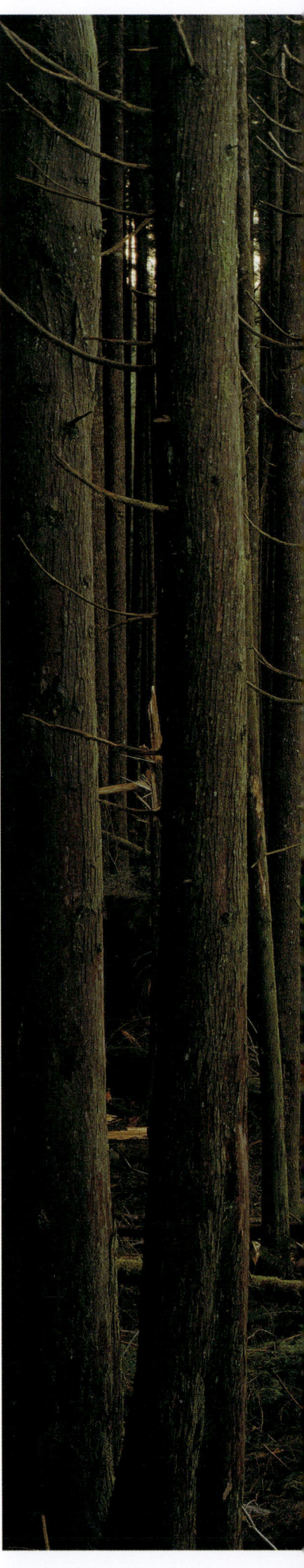

68   Freshly felled trees, Nemah, Washington

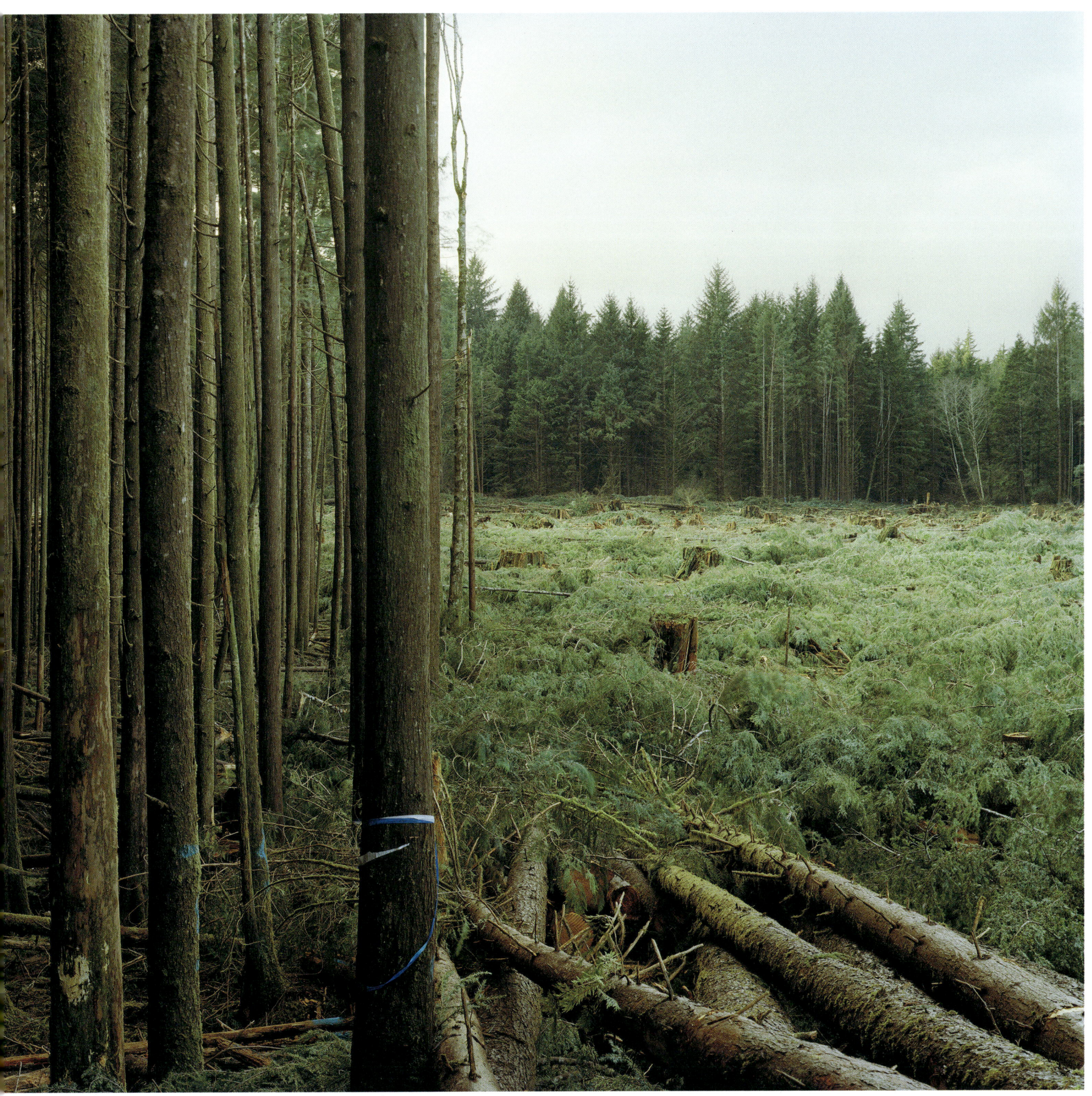

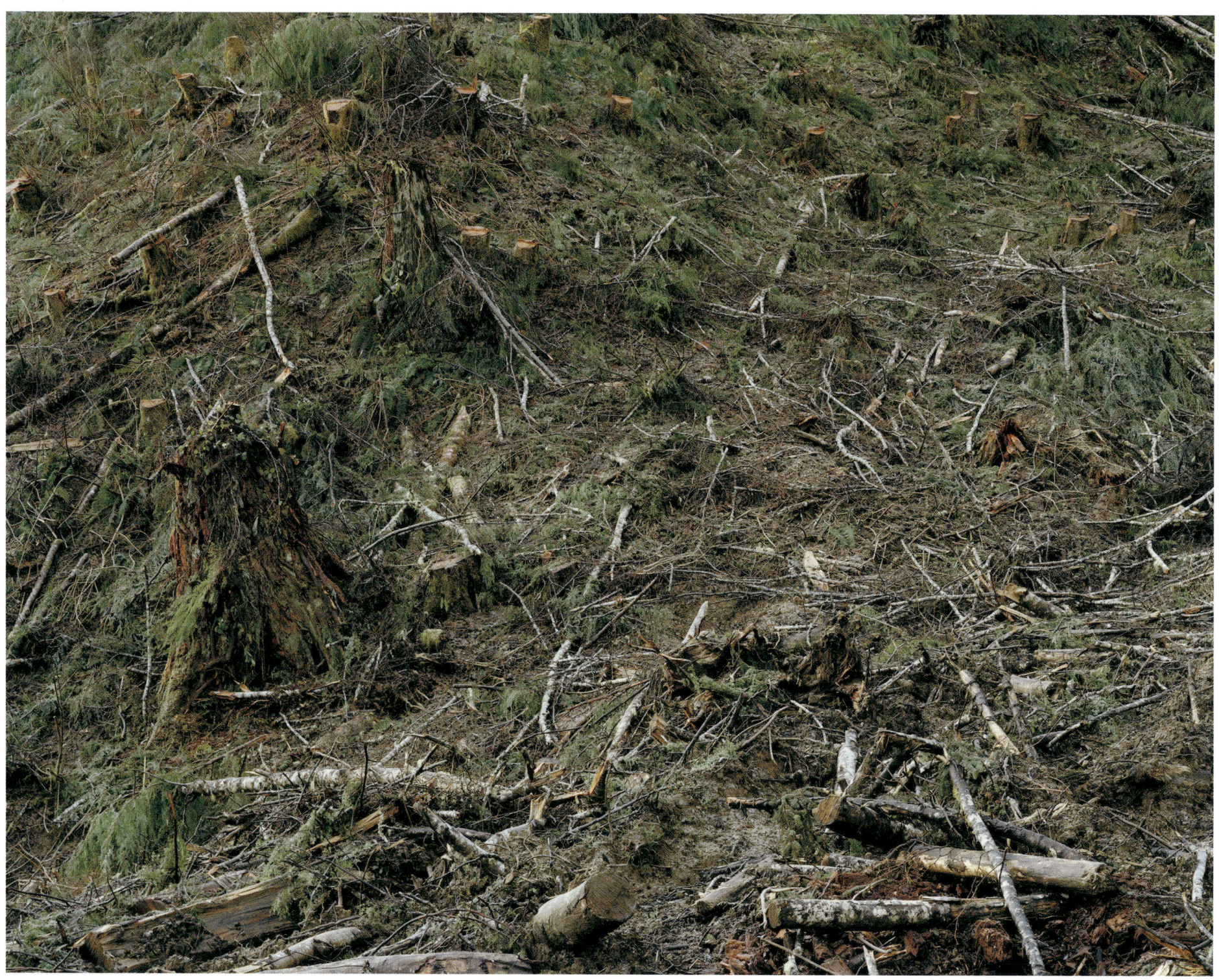

70   Clear-cut, Sekiu, Washington

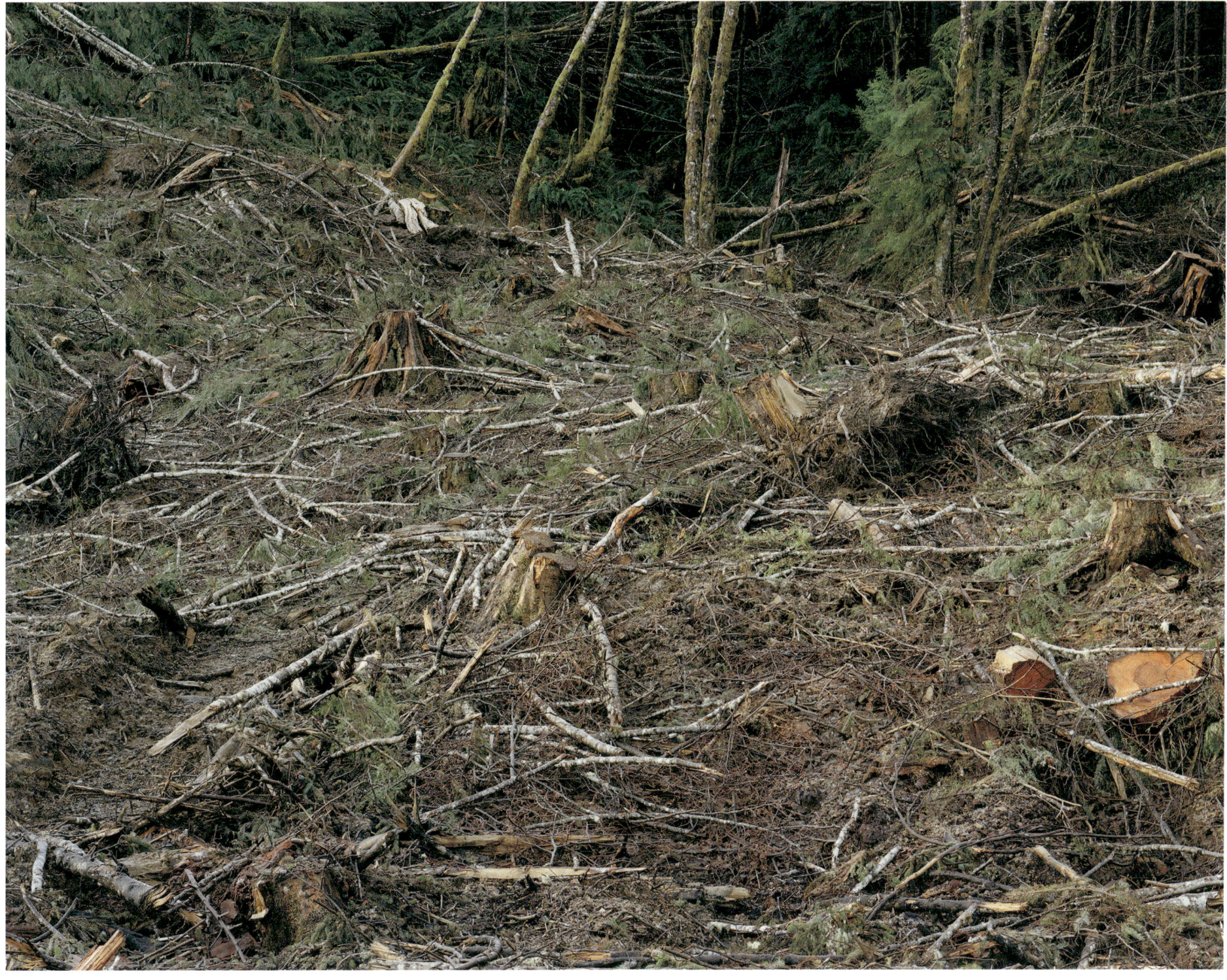

Power lines above Cosmopolis, Washington

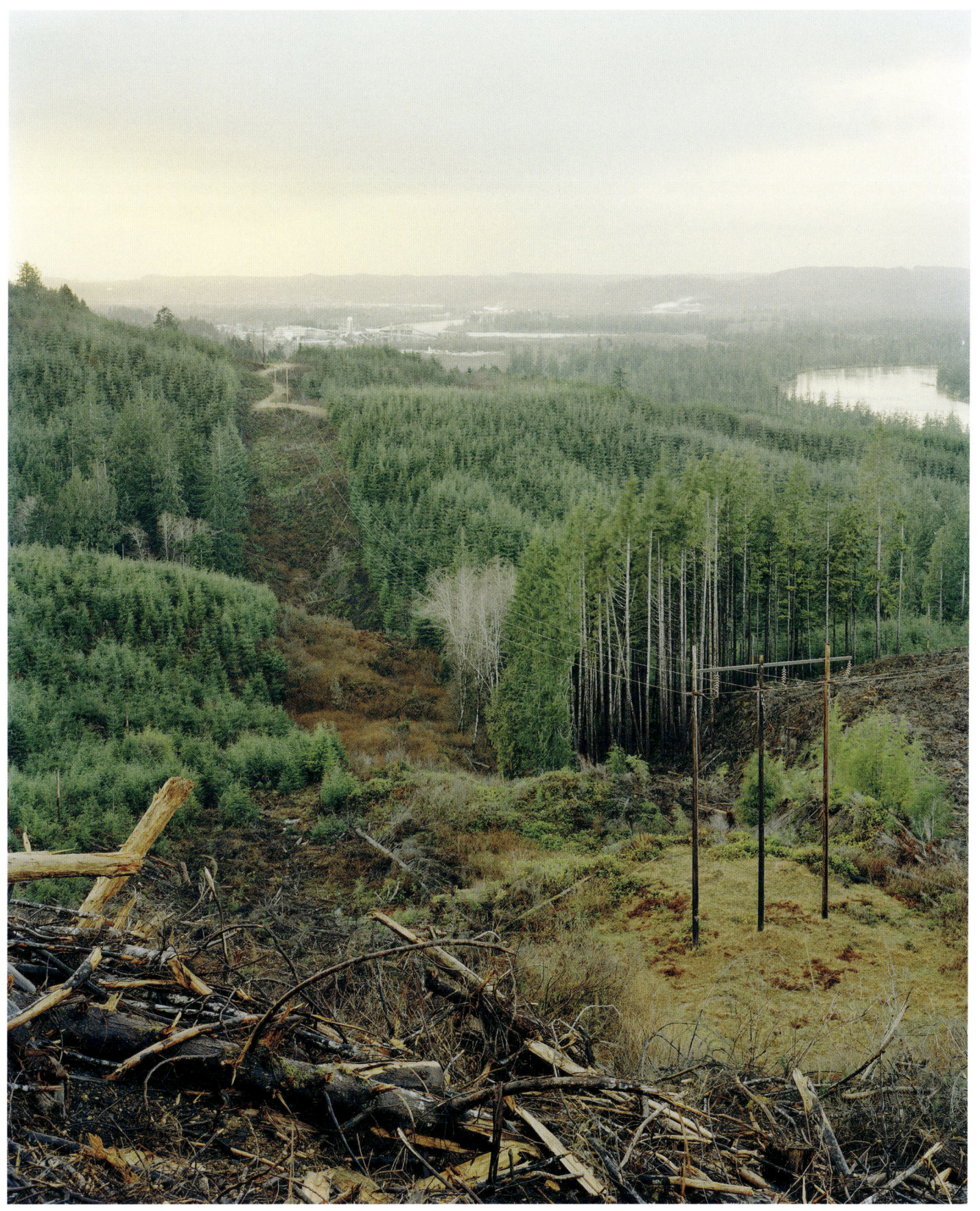

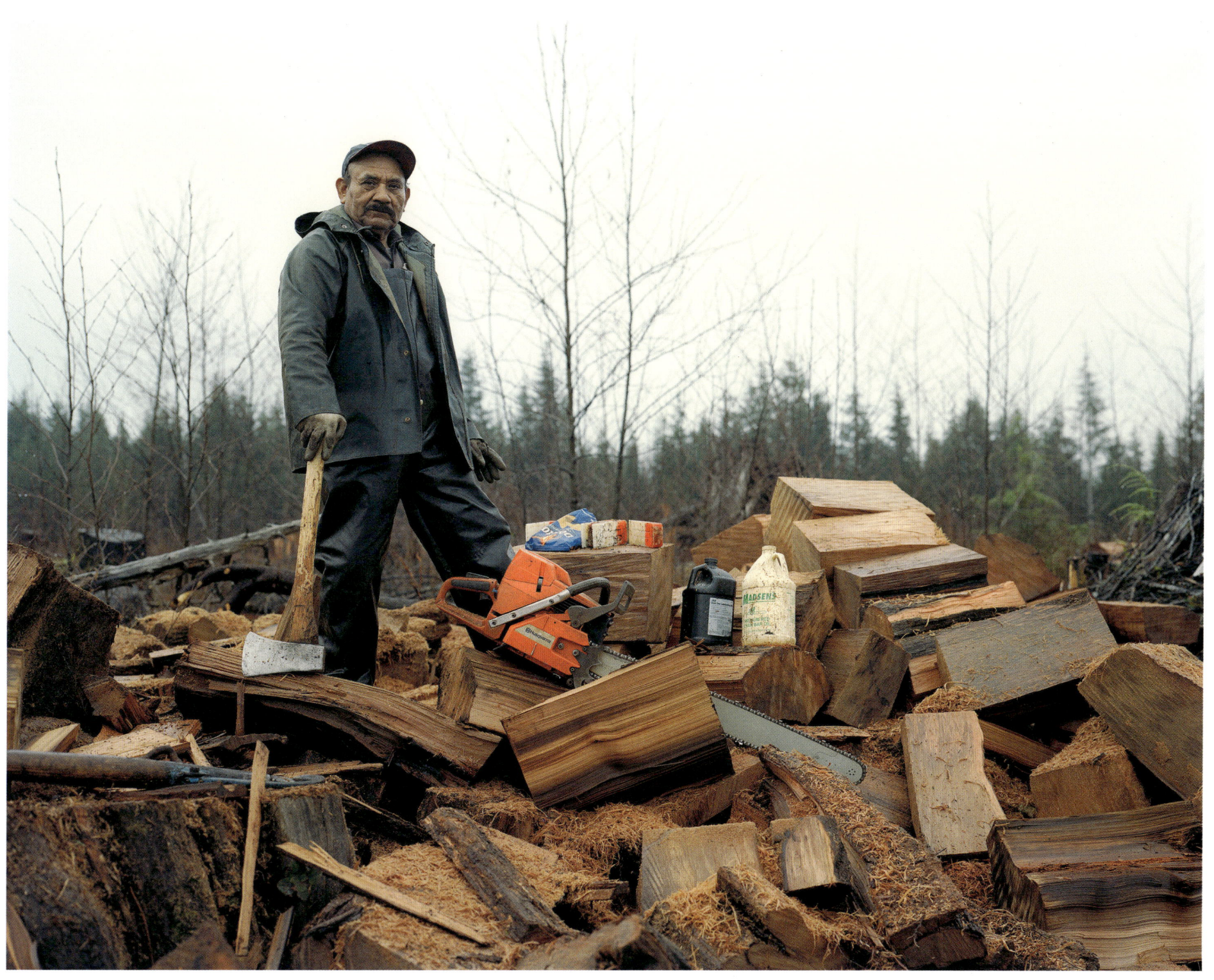

Juan Abalos, salvaging cedar shingle bolts, lower Hoh River, Washington   75

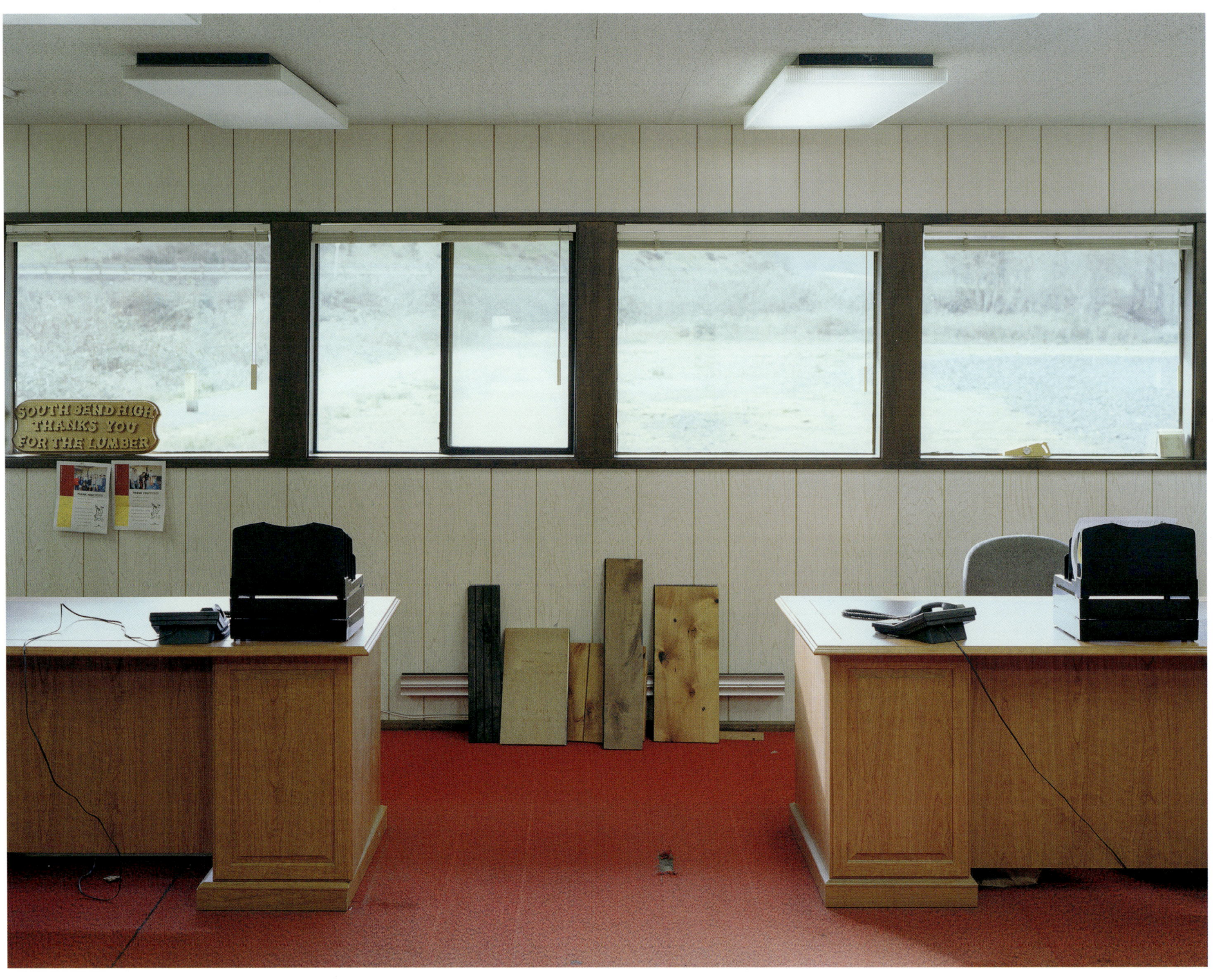

Offices, Seaport Lumber, South Bend, Washington

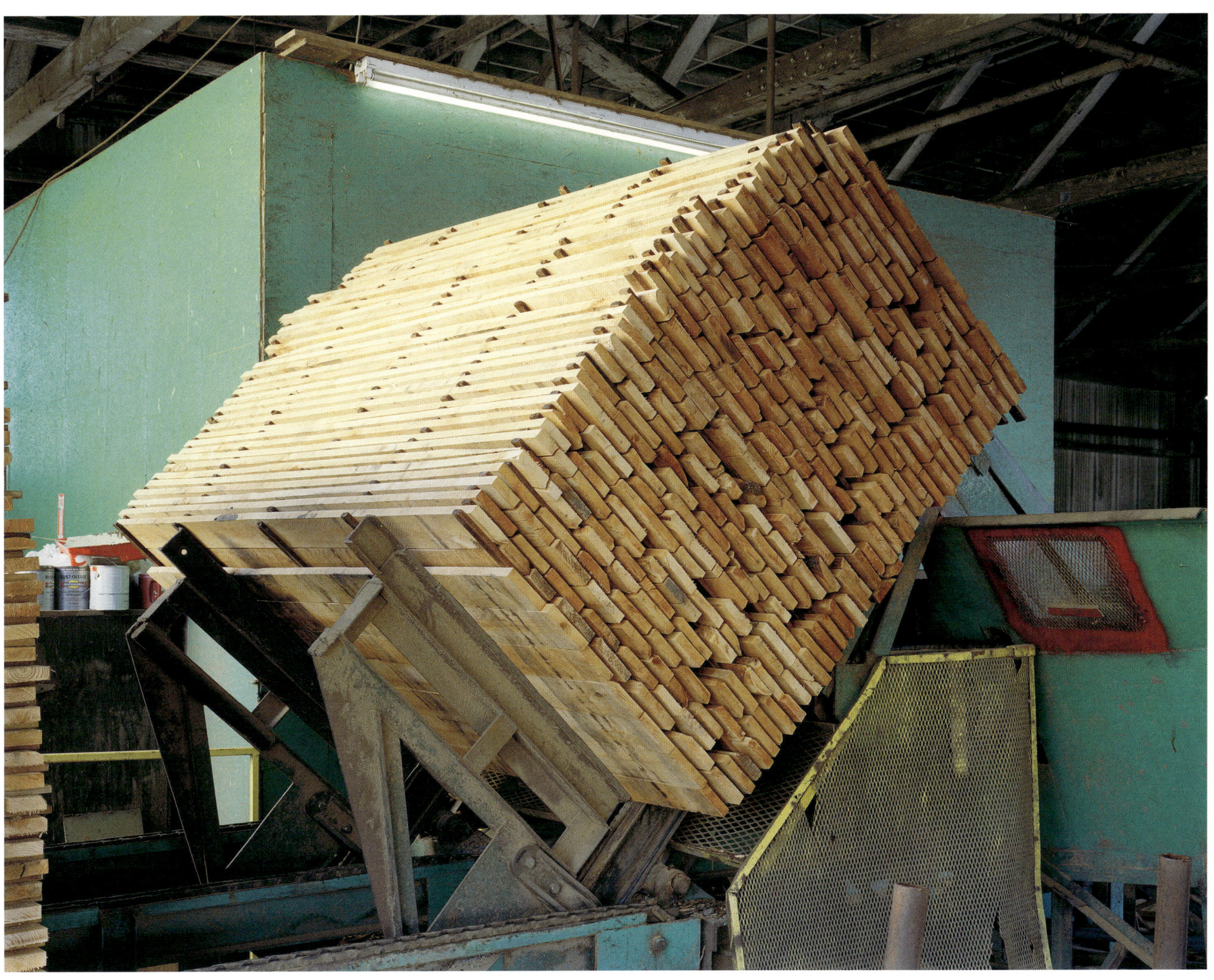

Stacked alder boards, Seaport Lumber, South Bend, Washington   77

Opposite: Sawdust, Seaport Lumber, South Bend, Washington;

78   *Following pages, left*: Old photograph, Seaport Lumber, South Bend, Washington; *right*: Juan Valencia, lower Hoh River, Washington

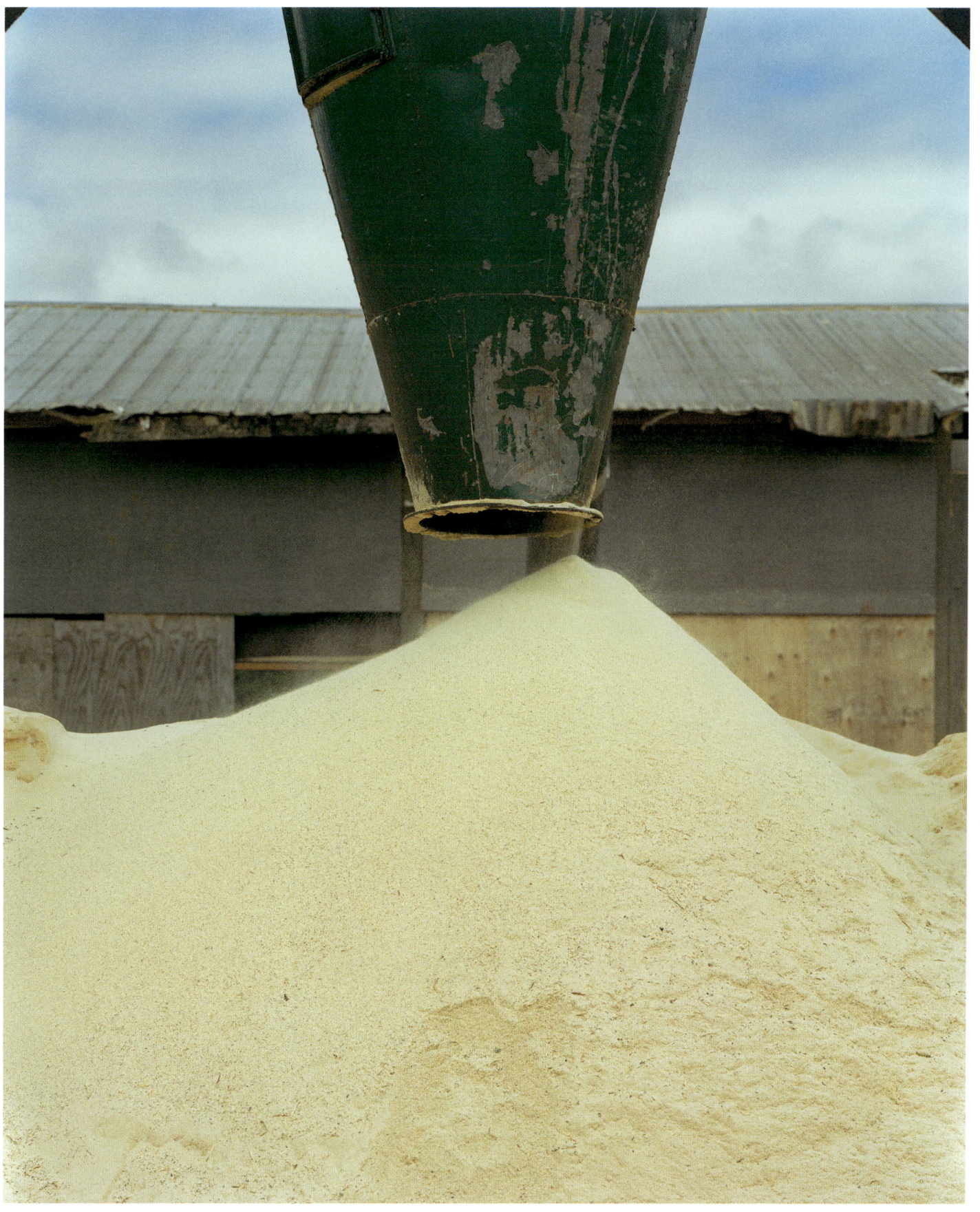

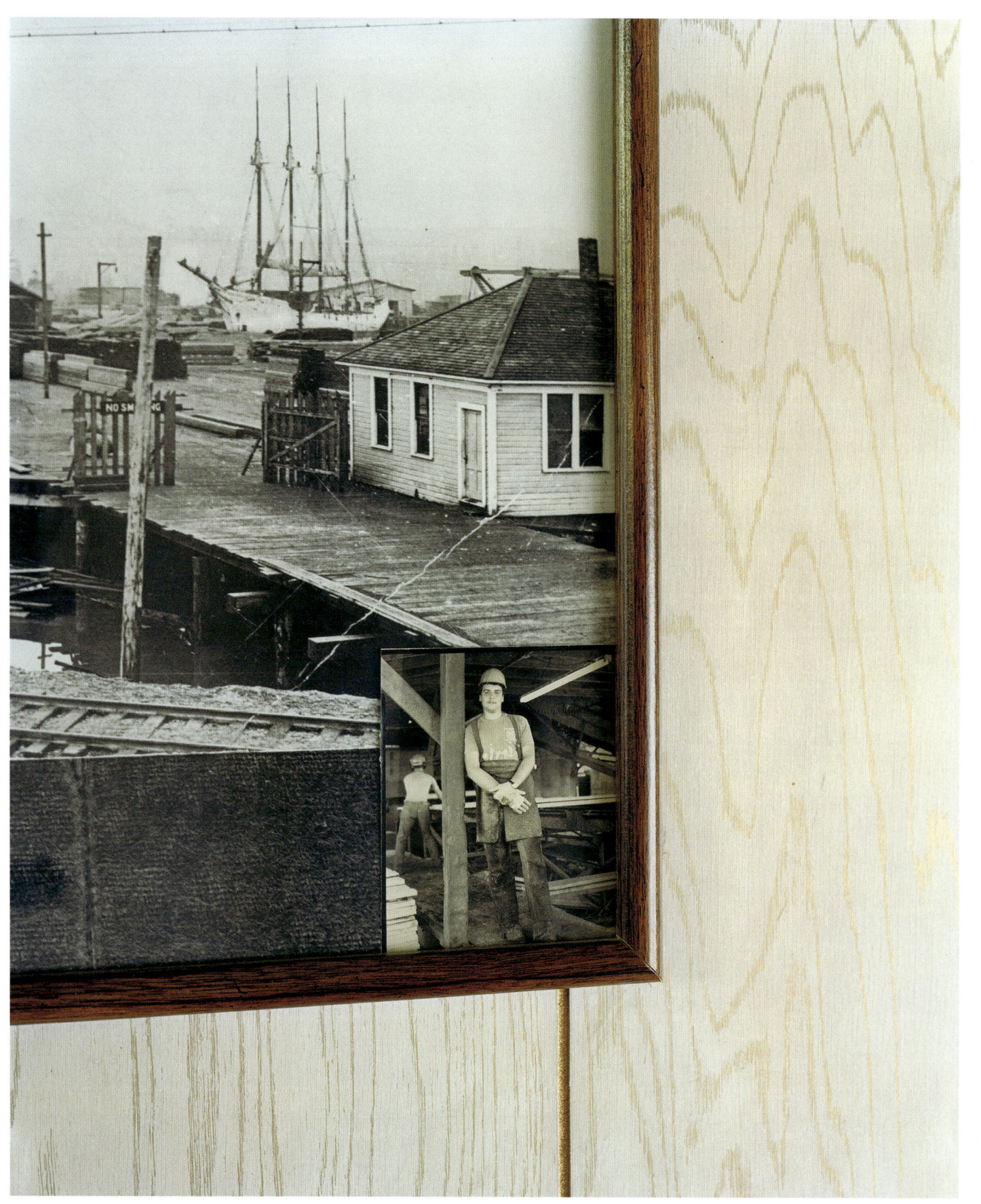

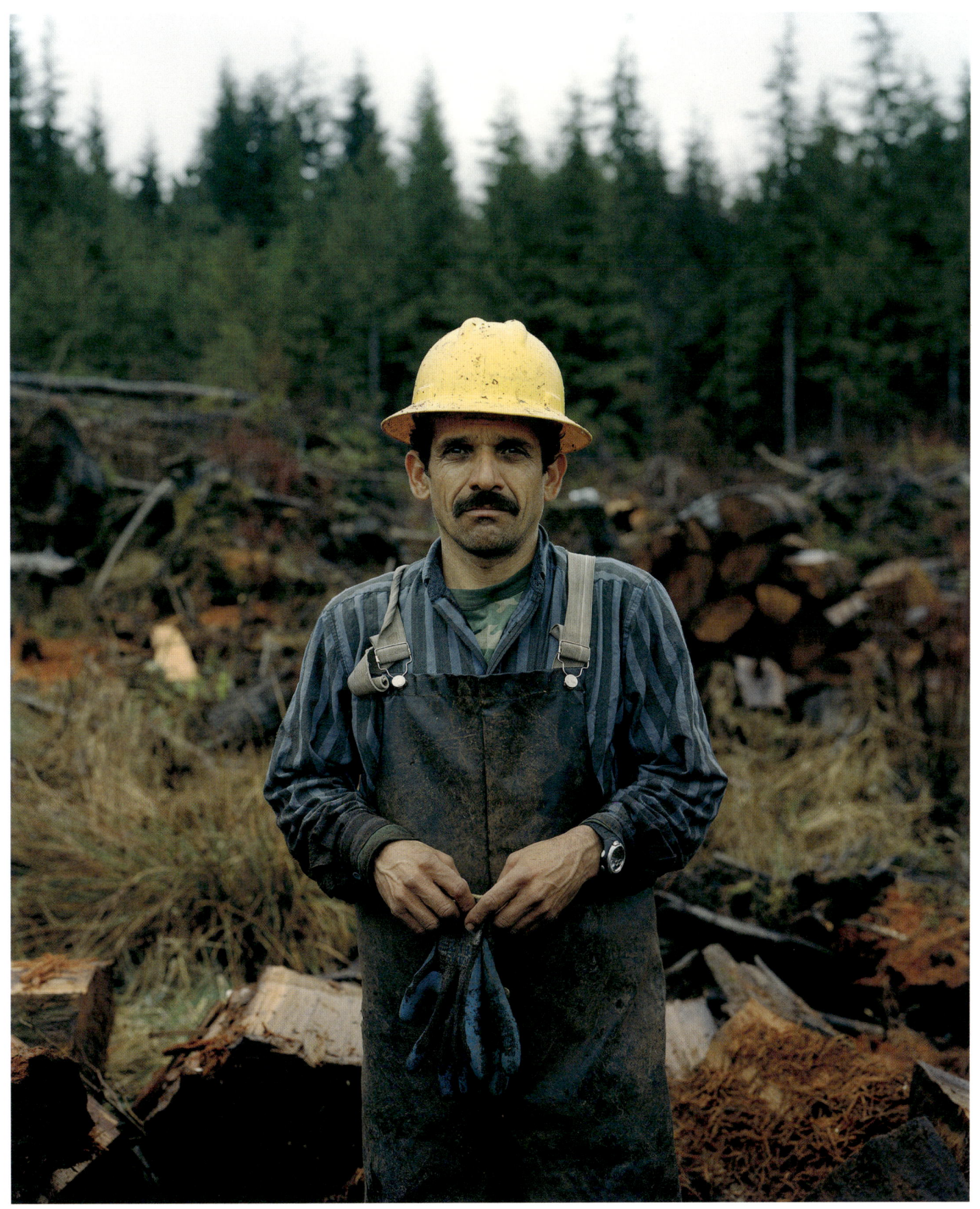

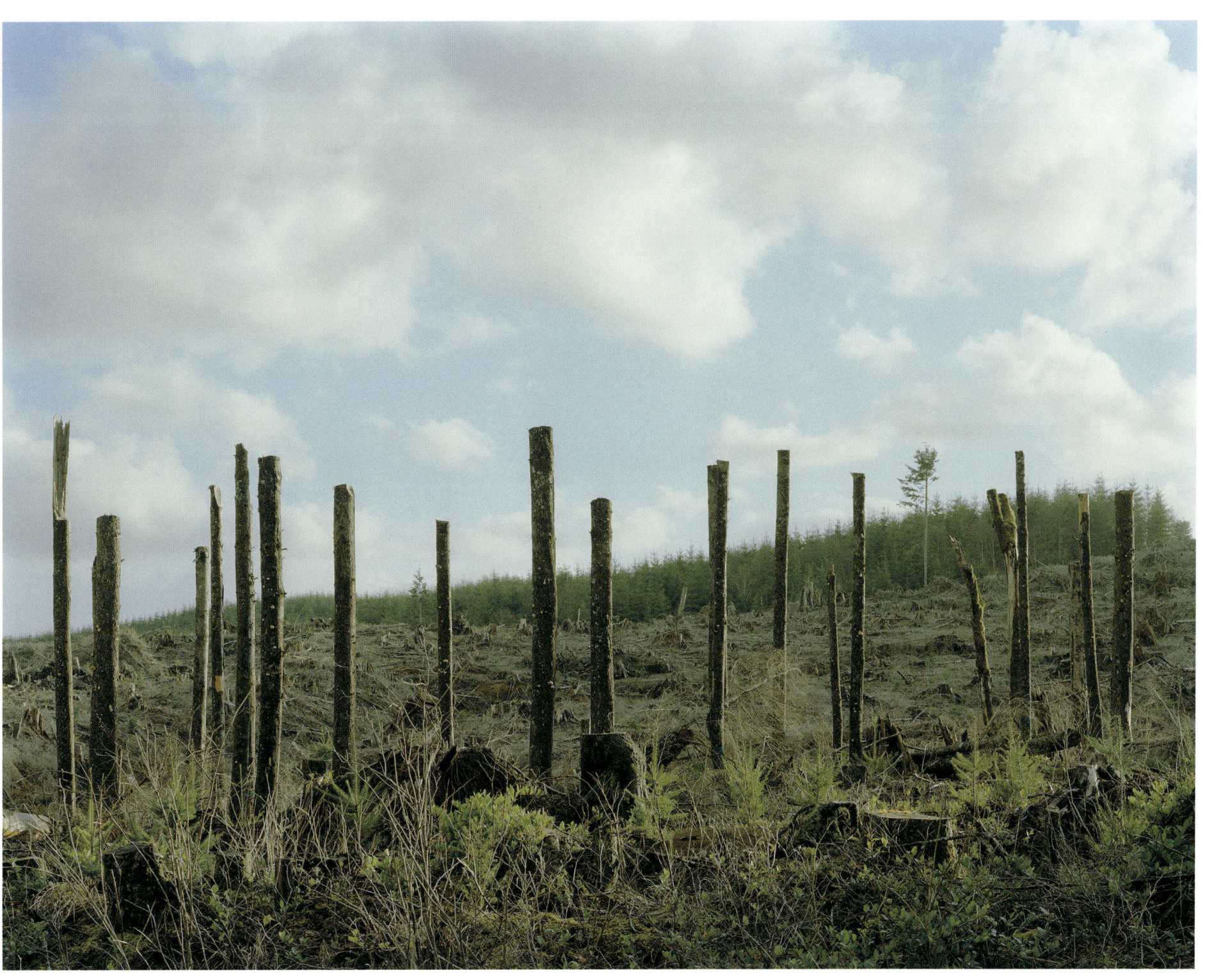

Topped trees reserved for wildlife, Nemah, Washington   83

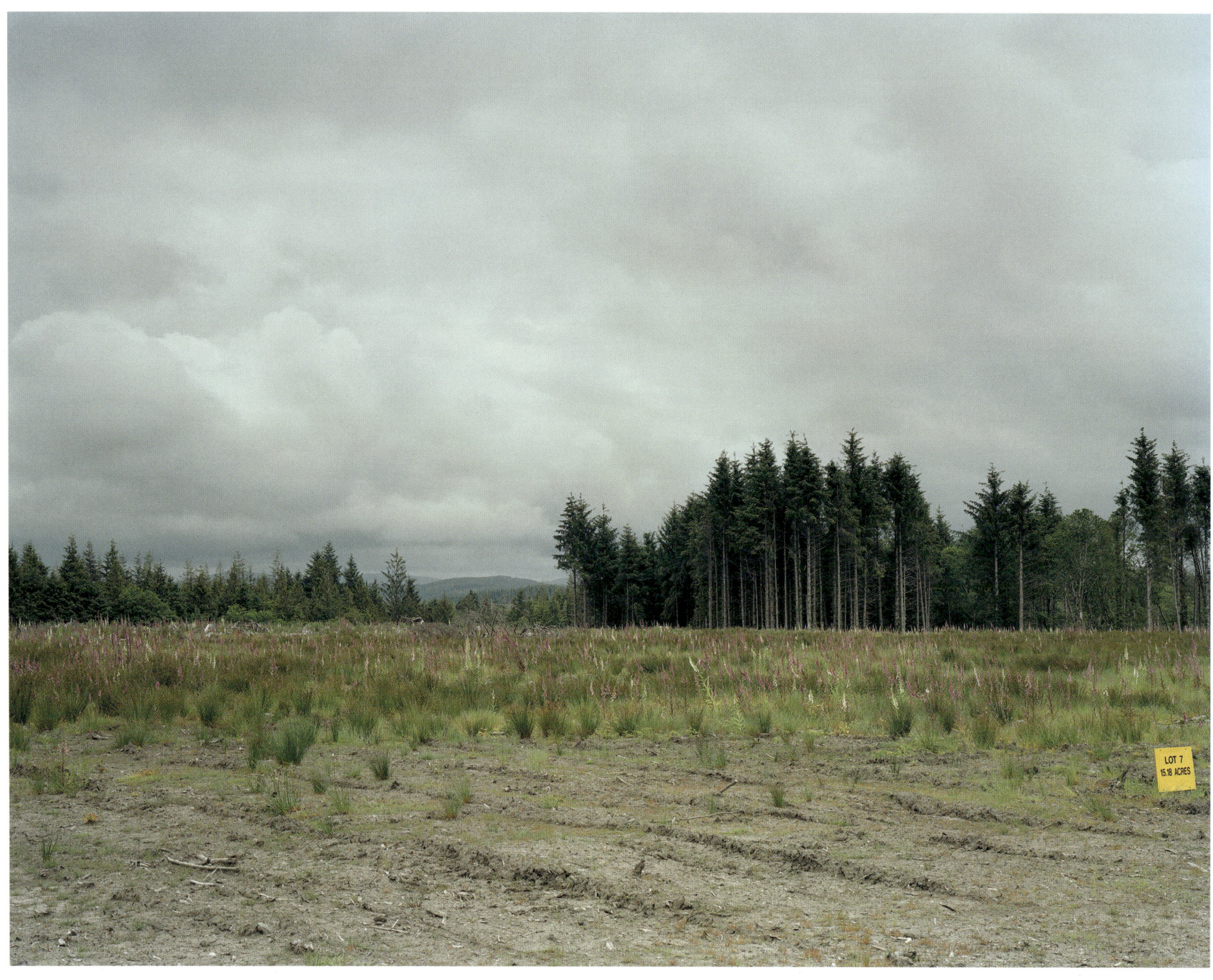

84   Willapa Sands Estates, South Bend, Washington

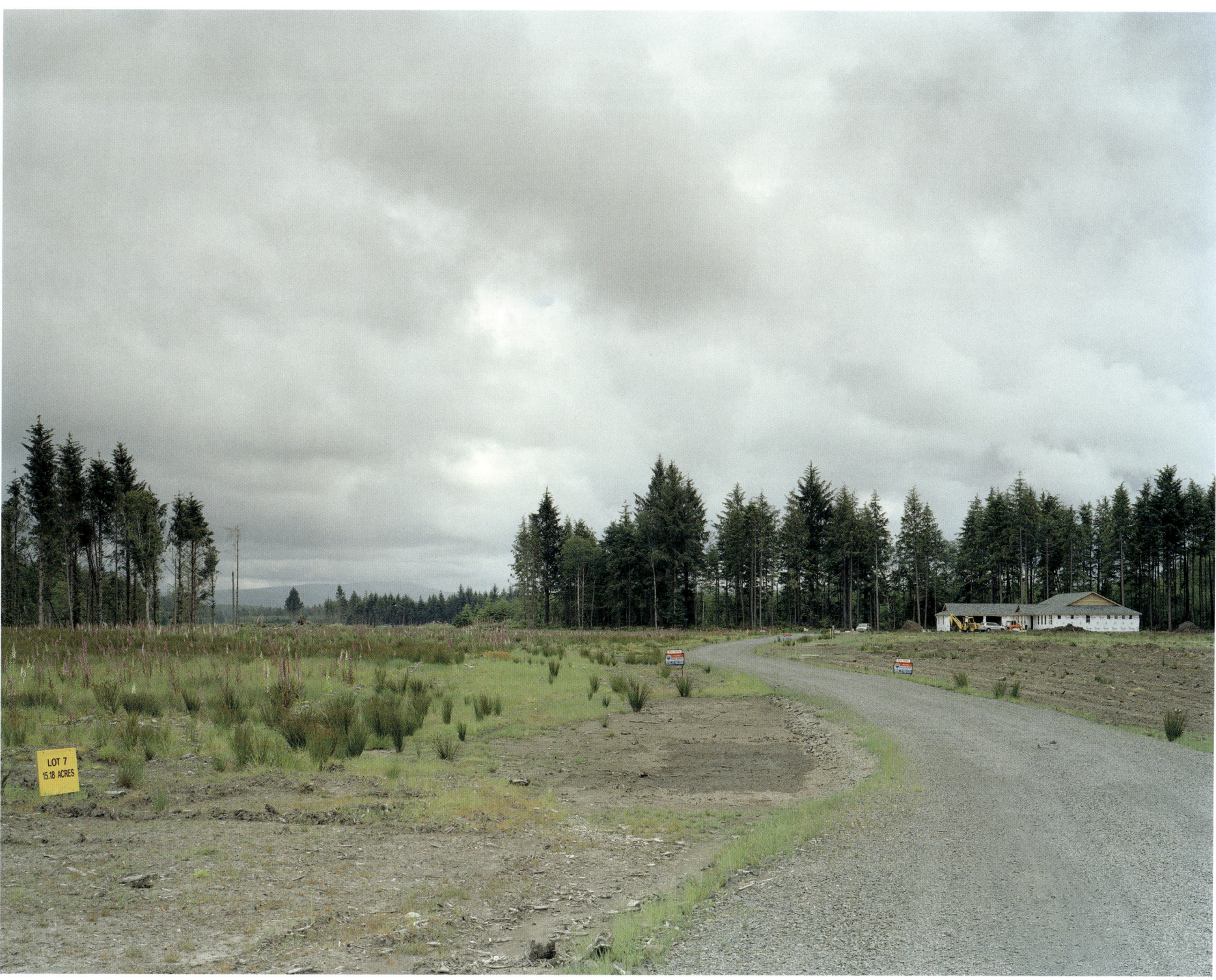

 Grays Harbor, Aberdeen, Washington

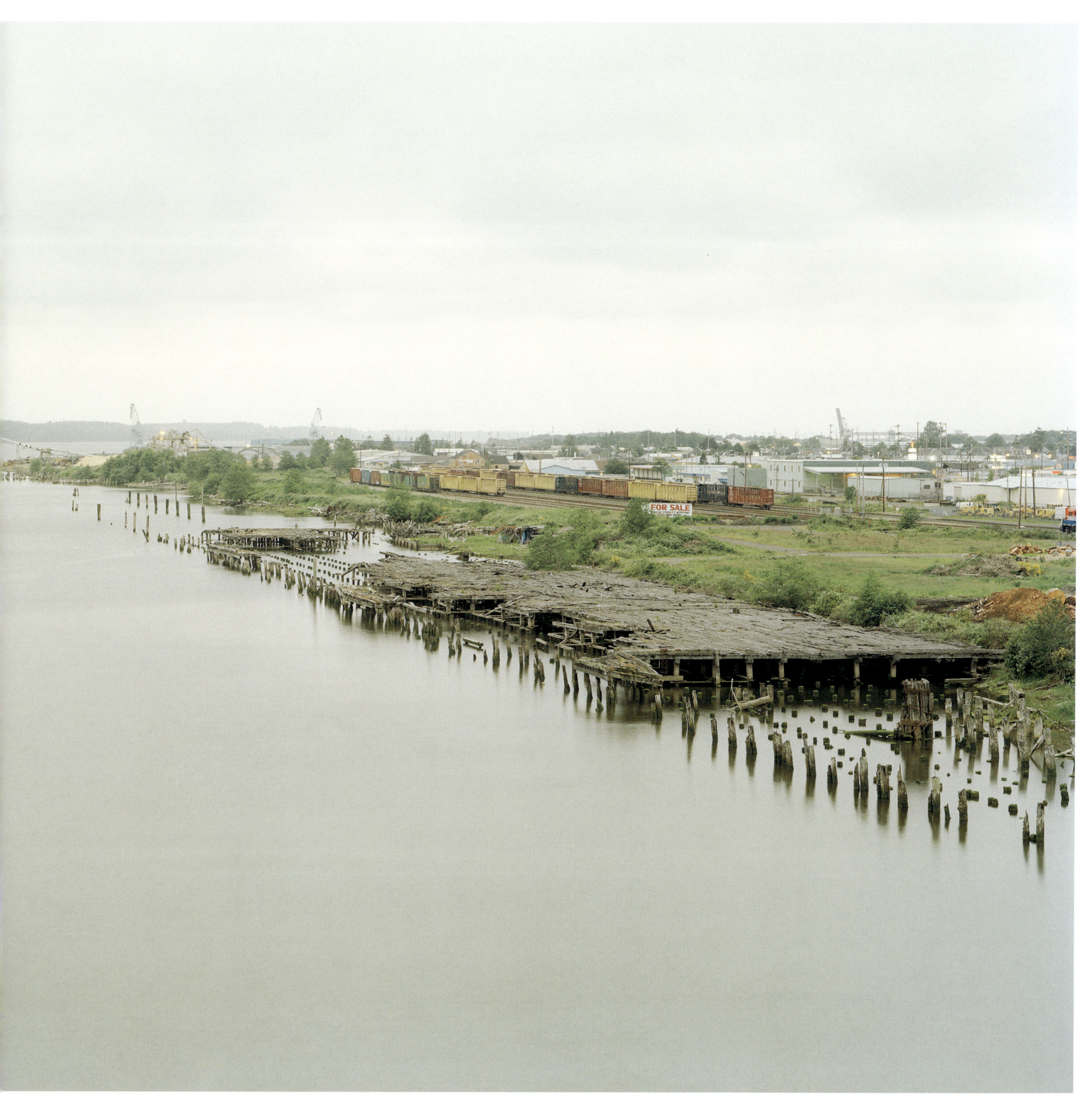

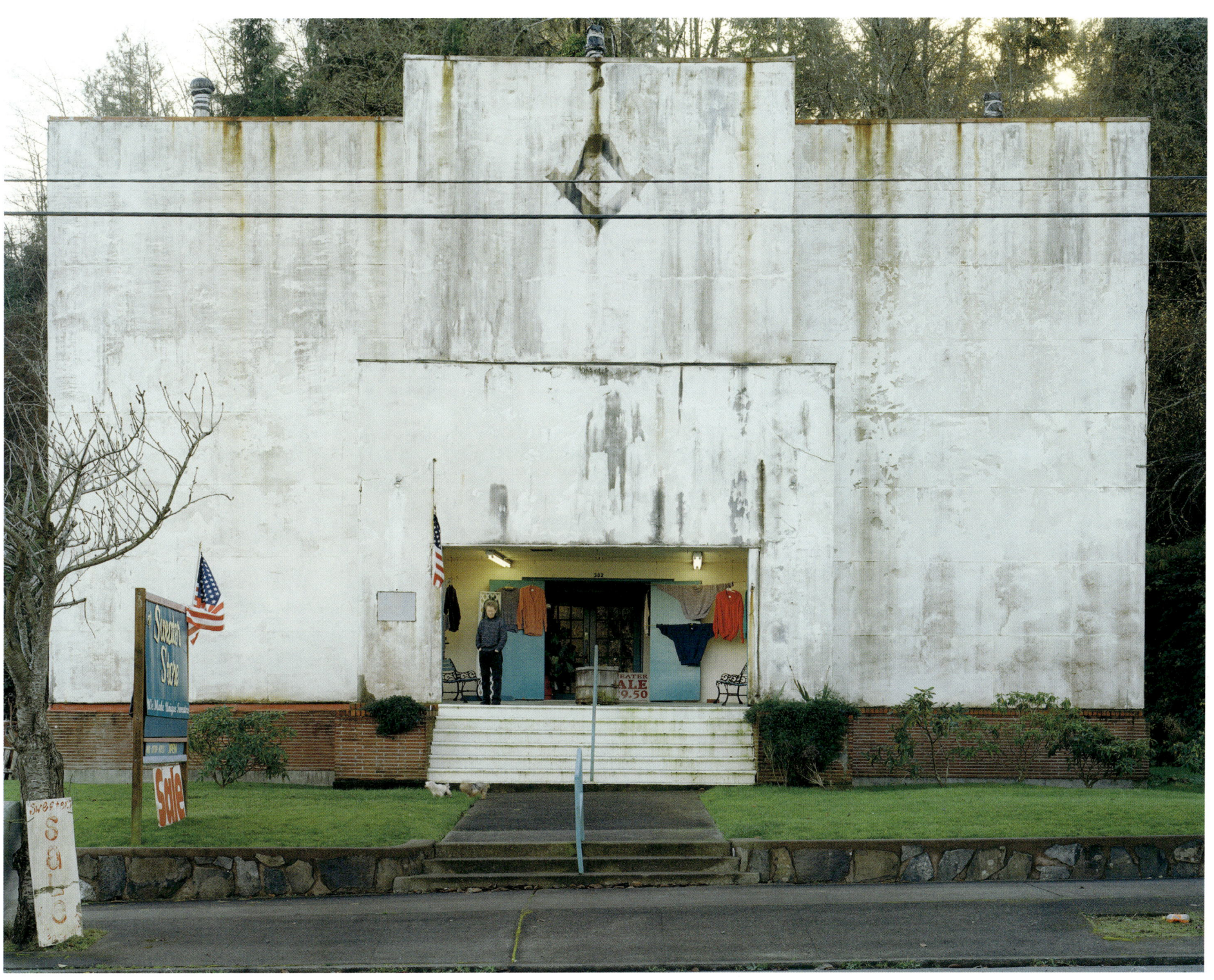

The Sweater Store, South Bend, Washington   89

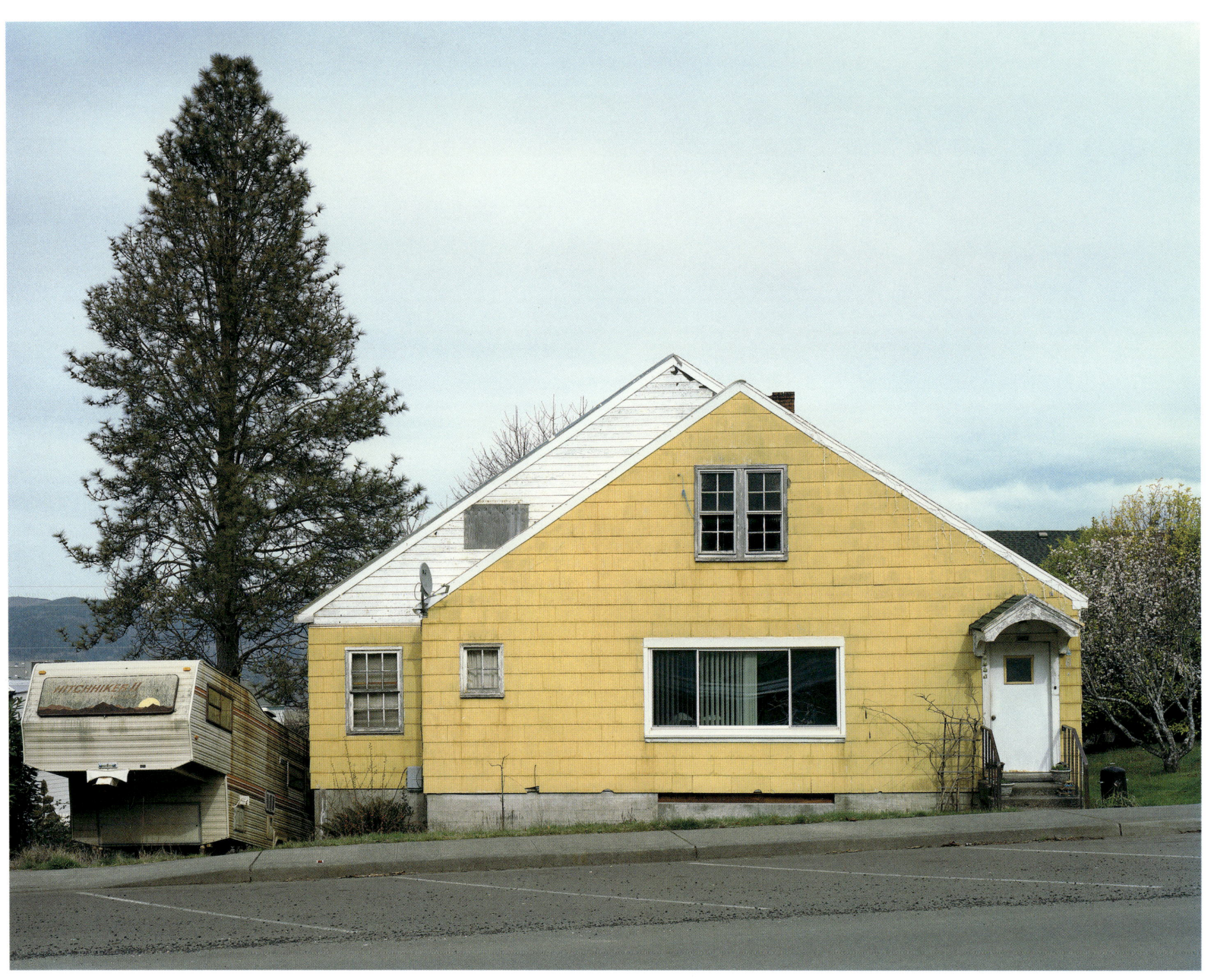

90   *Above*: South Bend, Washington; *Opposite:* Abandoned home, Arlington, Washington

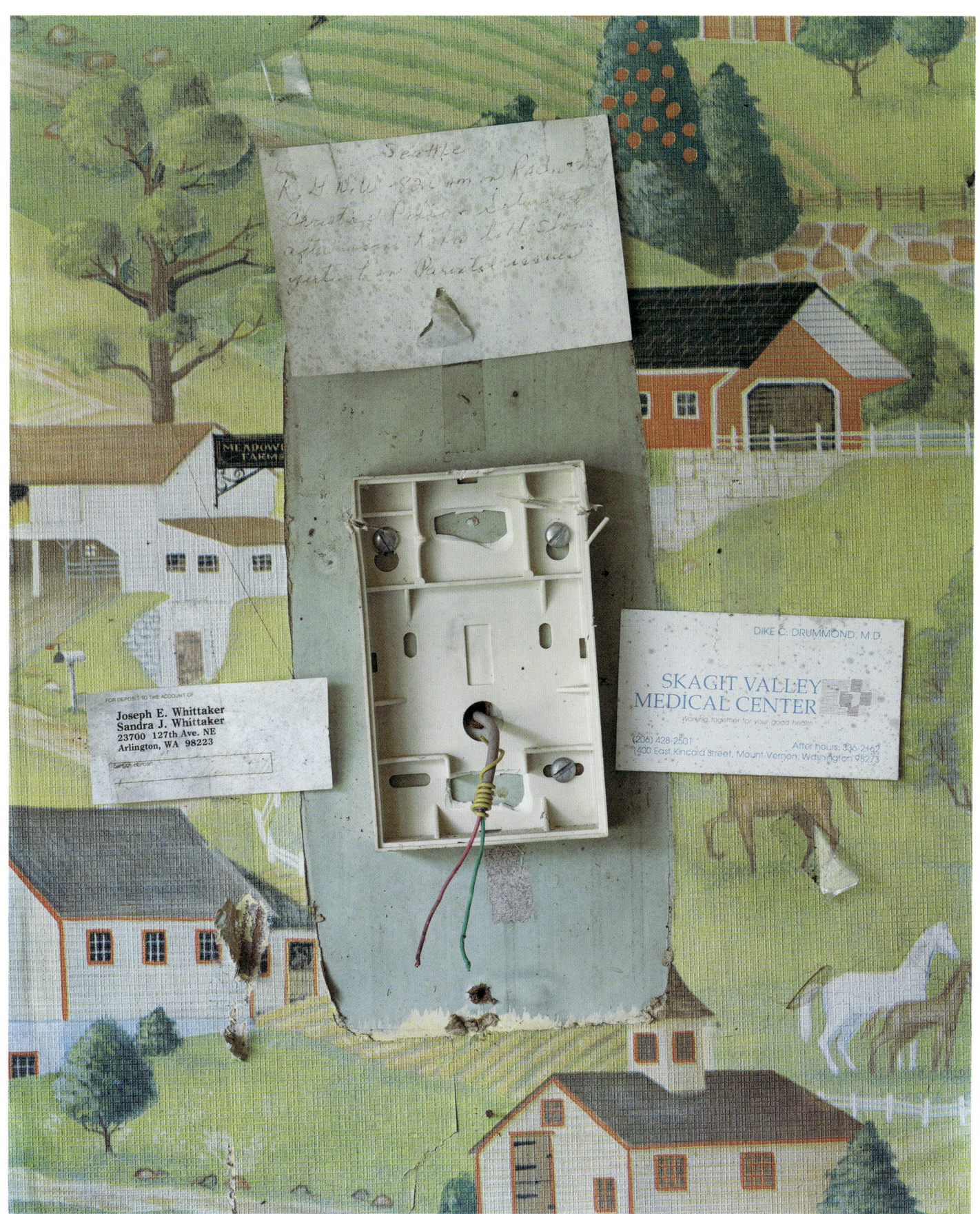

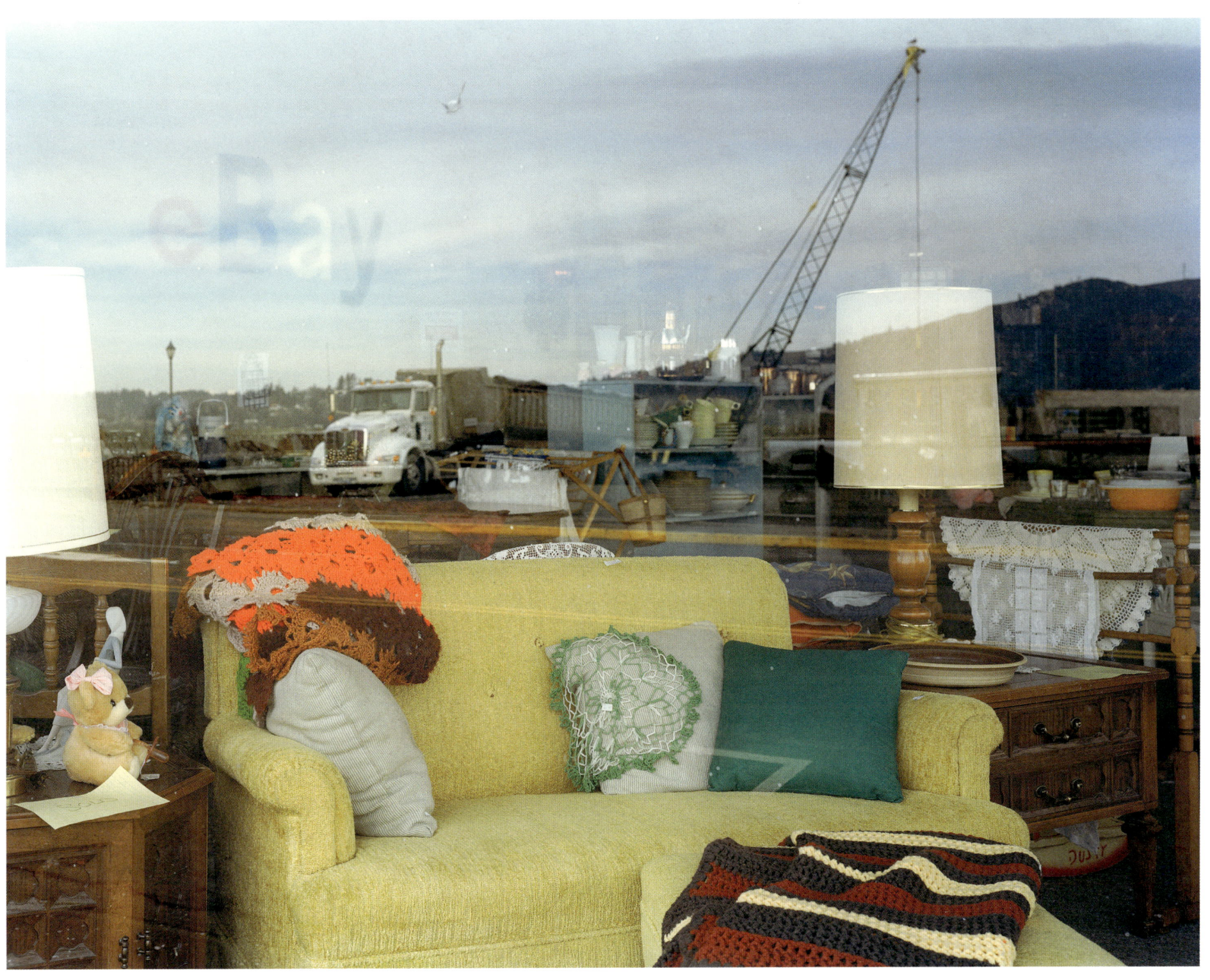

Just Sell It Now on eBay consignment store, South Bend, Washington   93

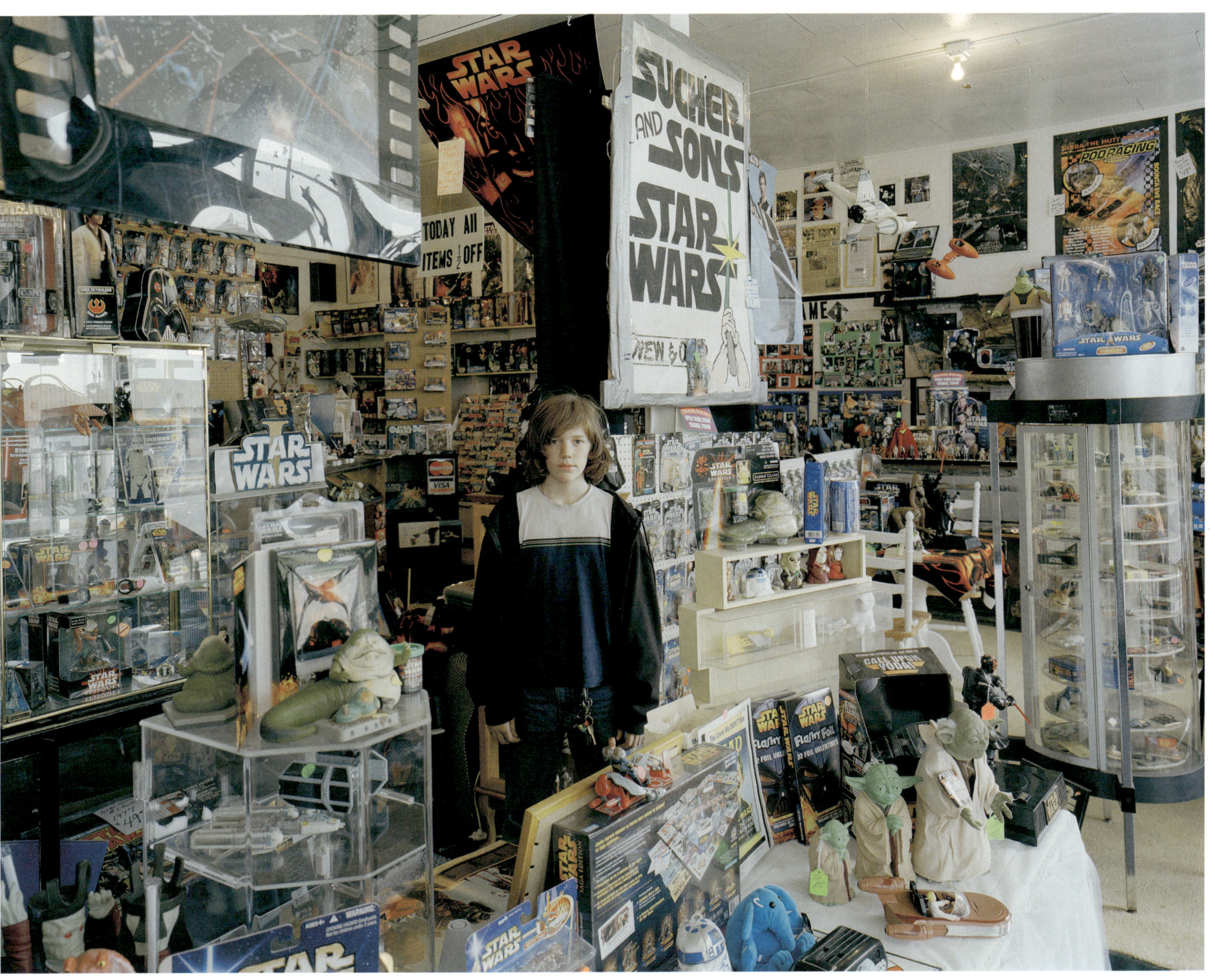

Colin Sucher & Sons Star Wars store, Aberdeen, Washington   95

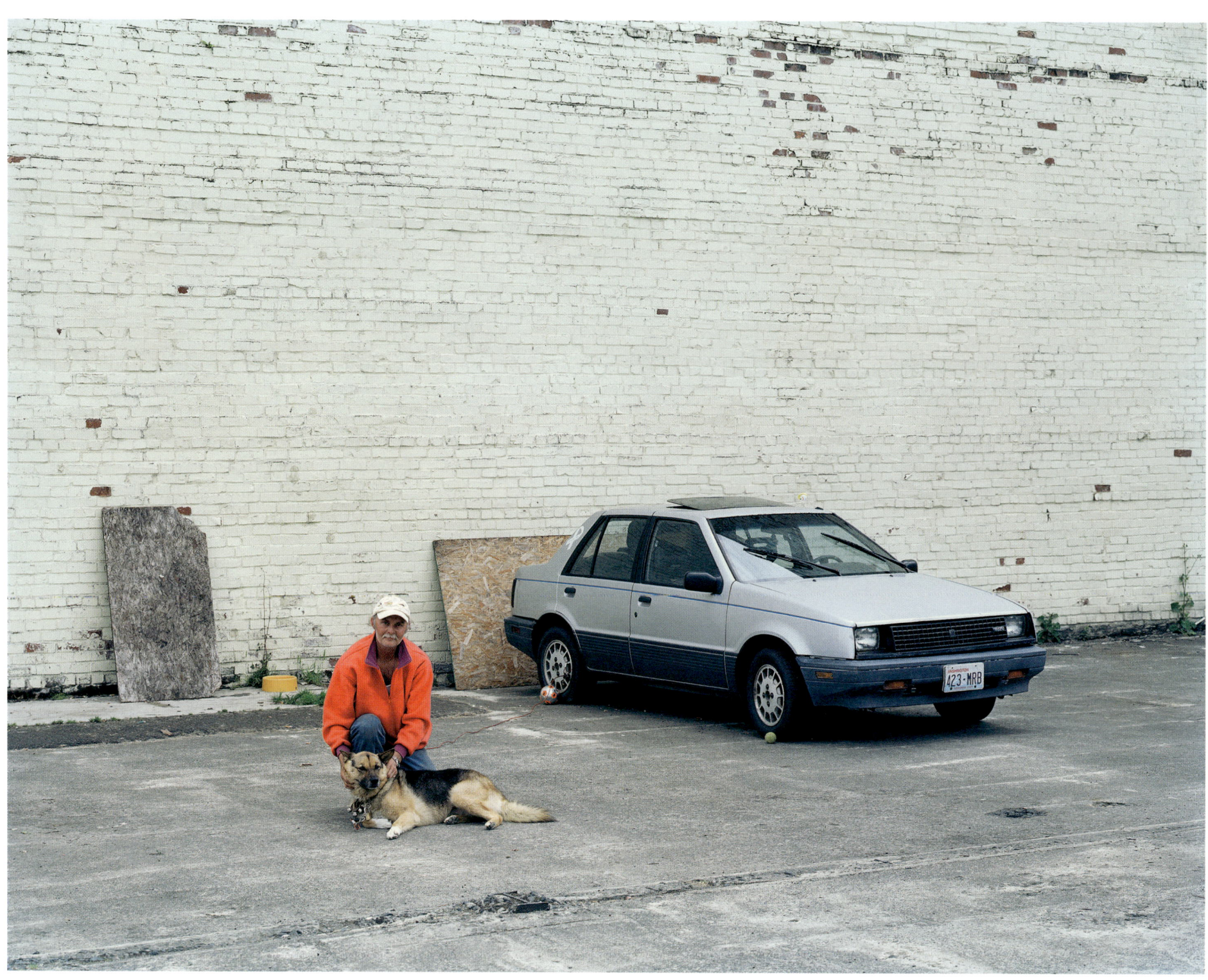

96   Jim and Star, Aberdeen, Washington

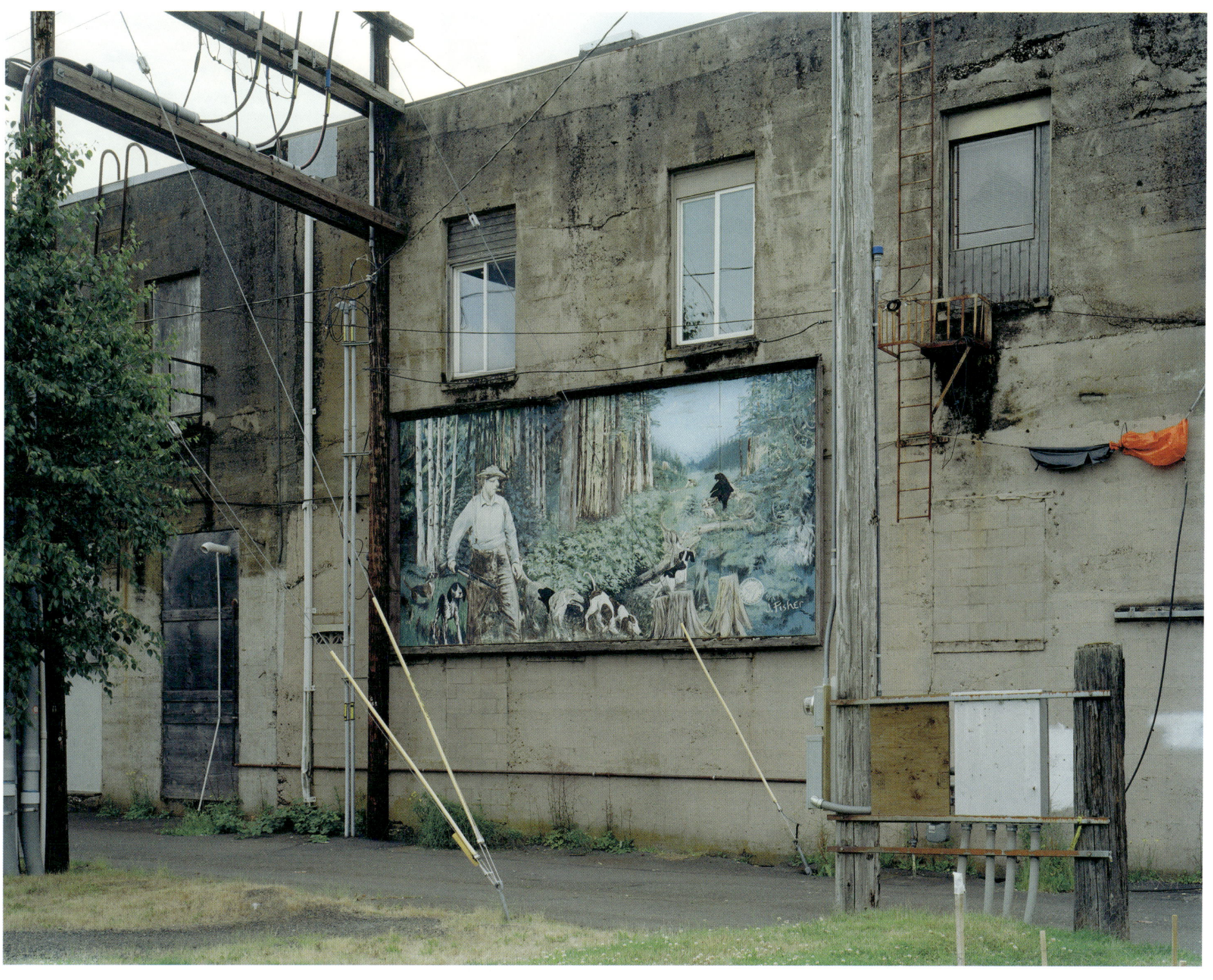

Alley mural, Aberdeen, Washington　97

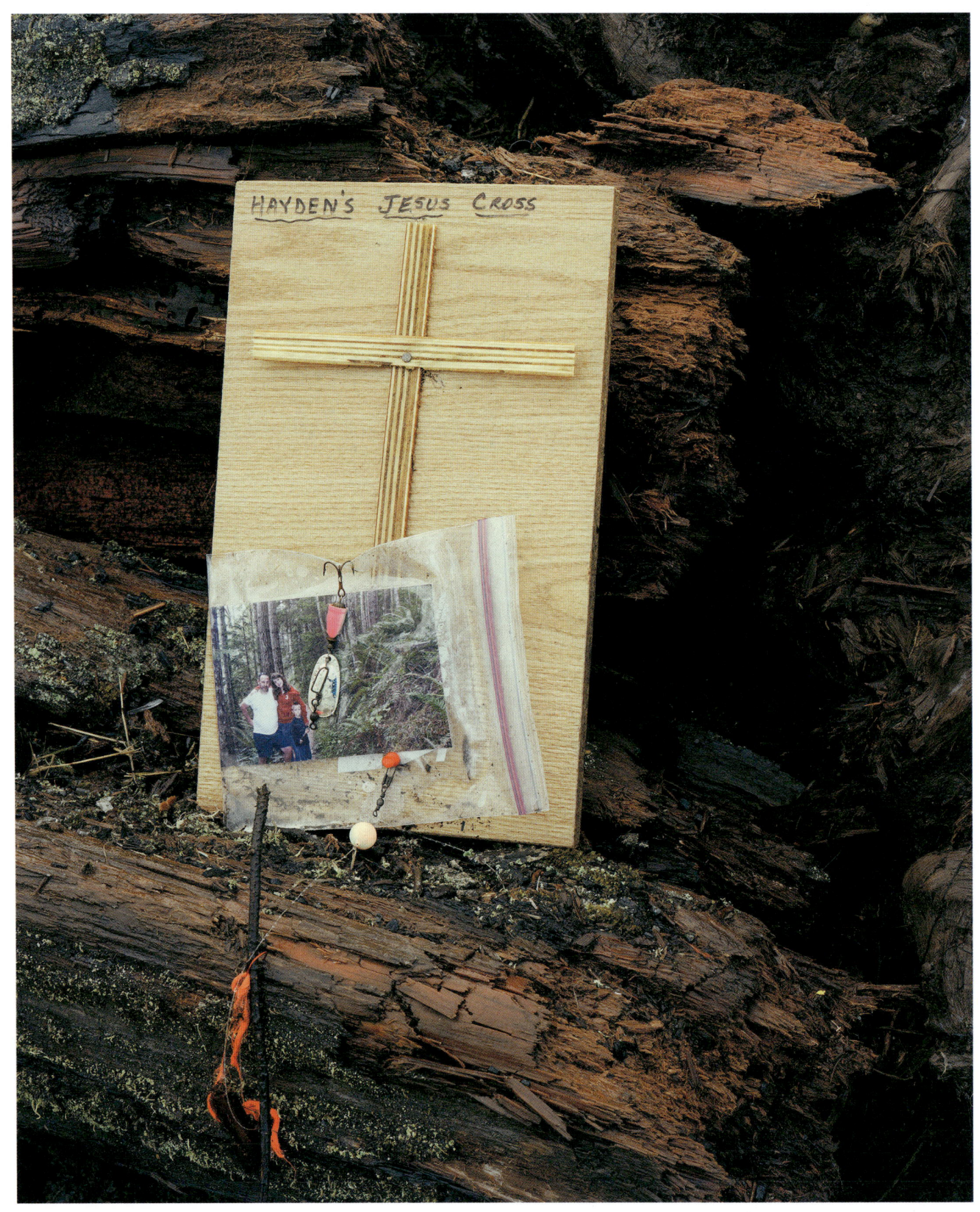

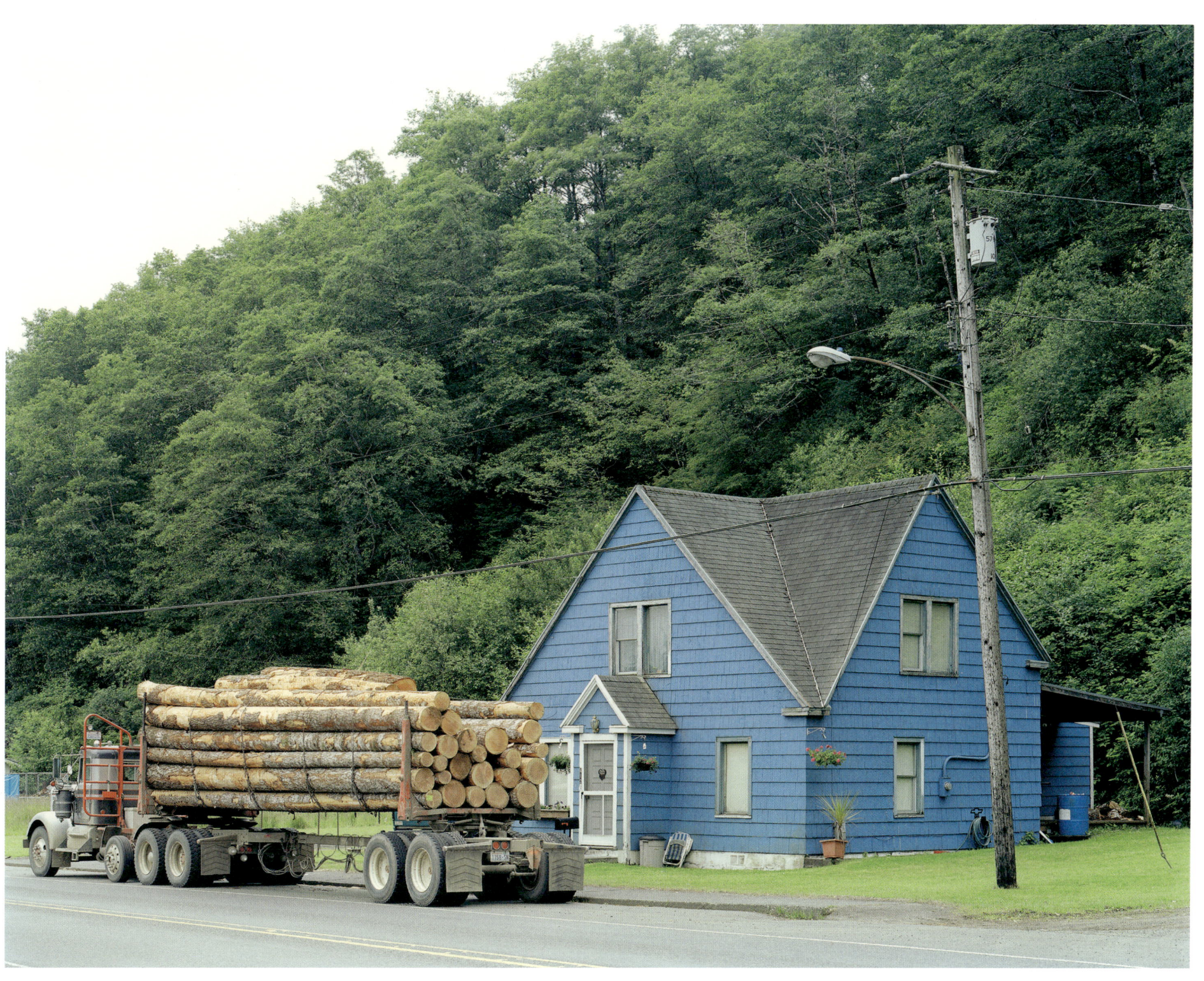

Opposite: Memorial outside Joyce, Washington; *Above*: Hoquiam, Washington   99

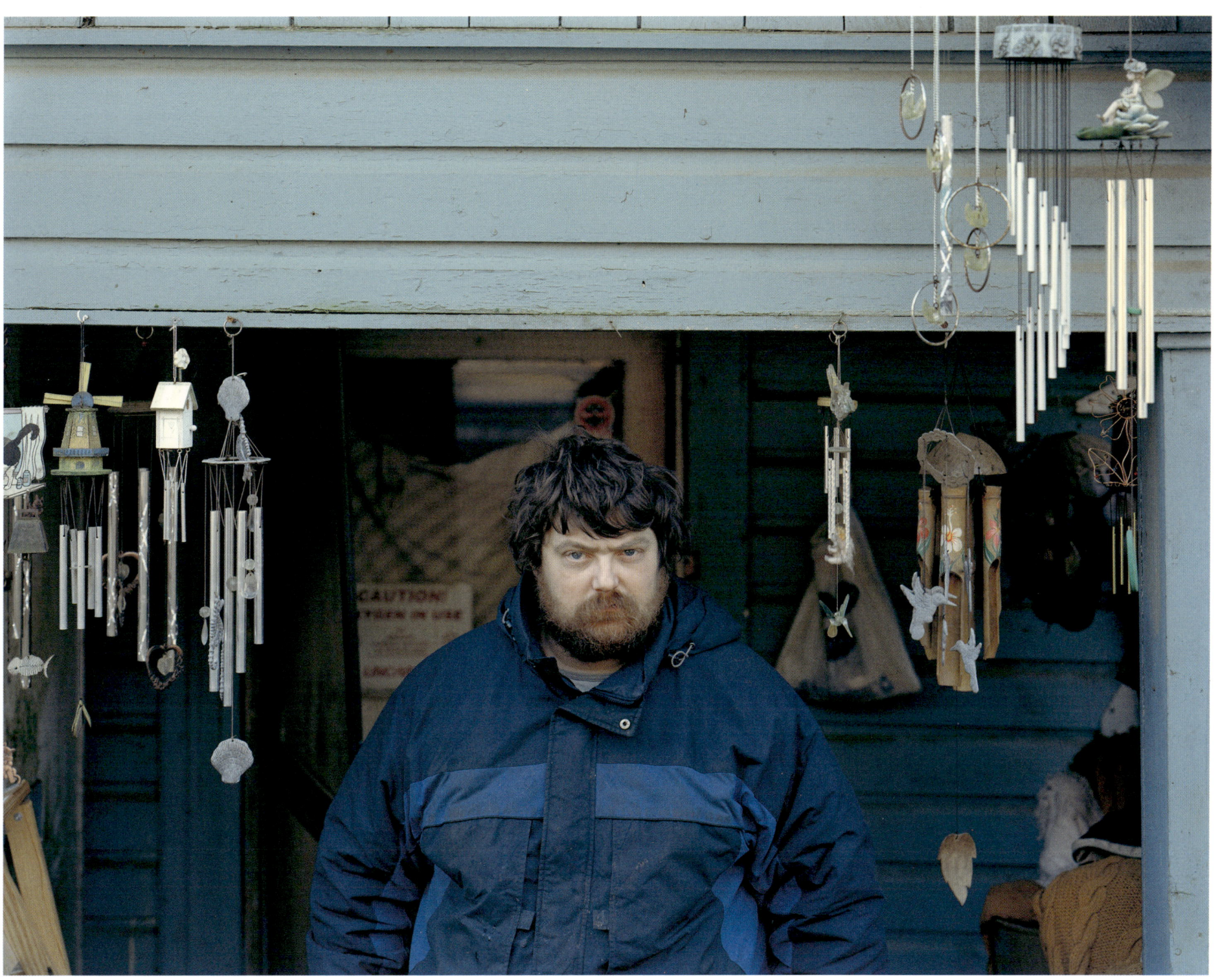

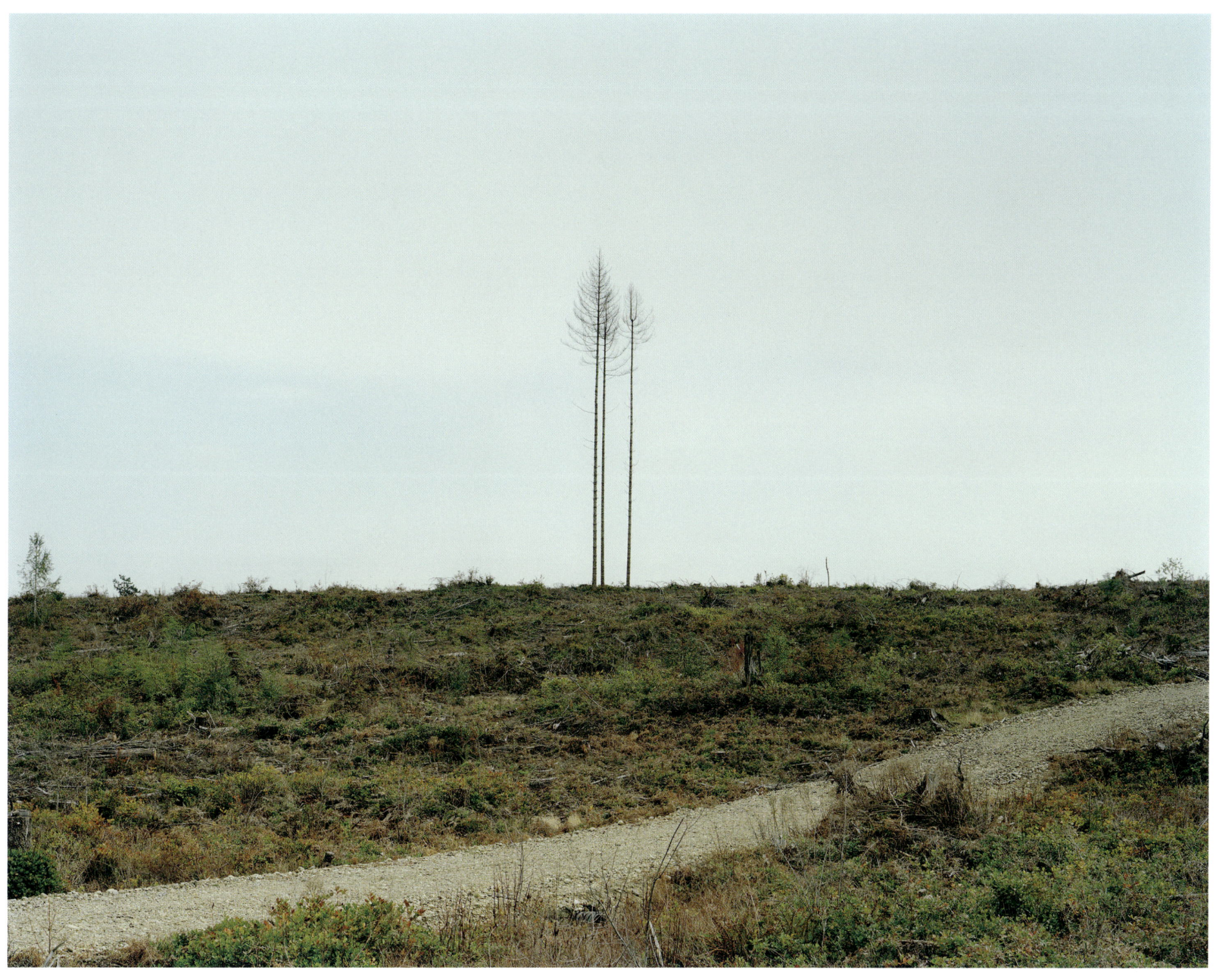

Logging road near Shelton, Washington   103

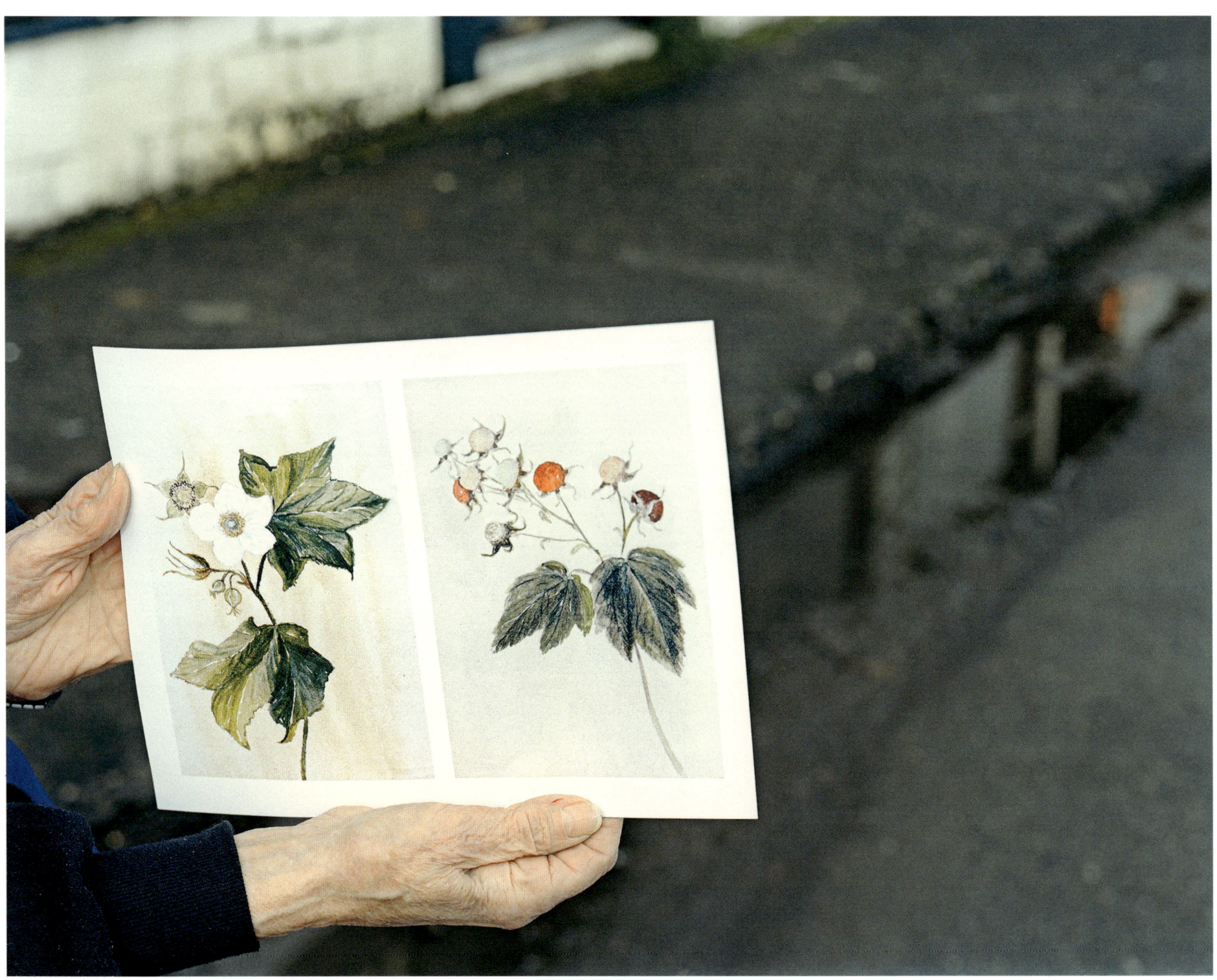

104   Missy with wildflower watercolors, Forks, Washington

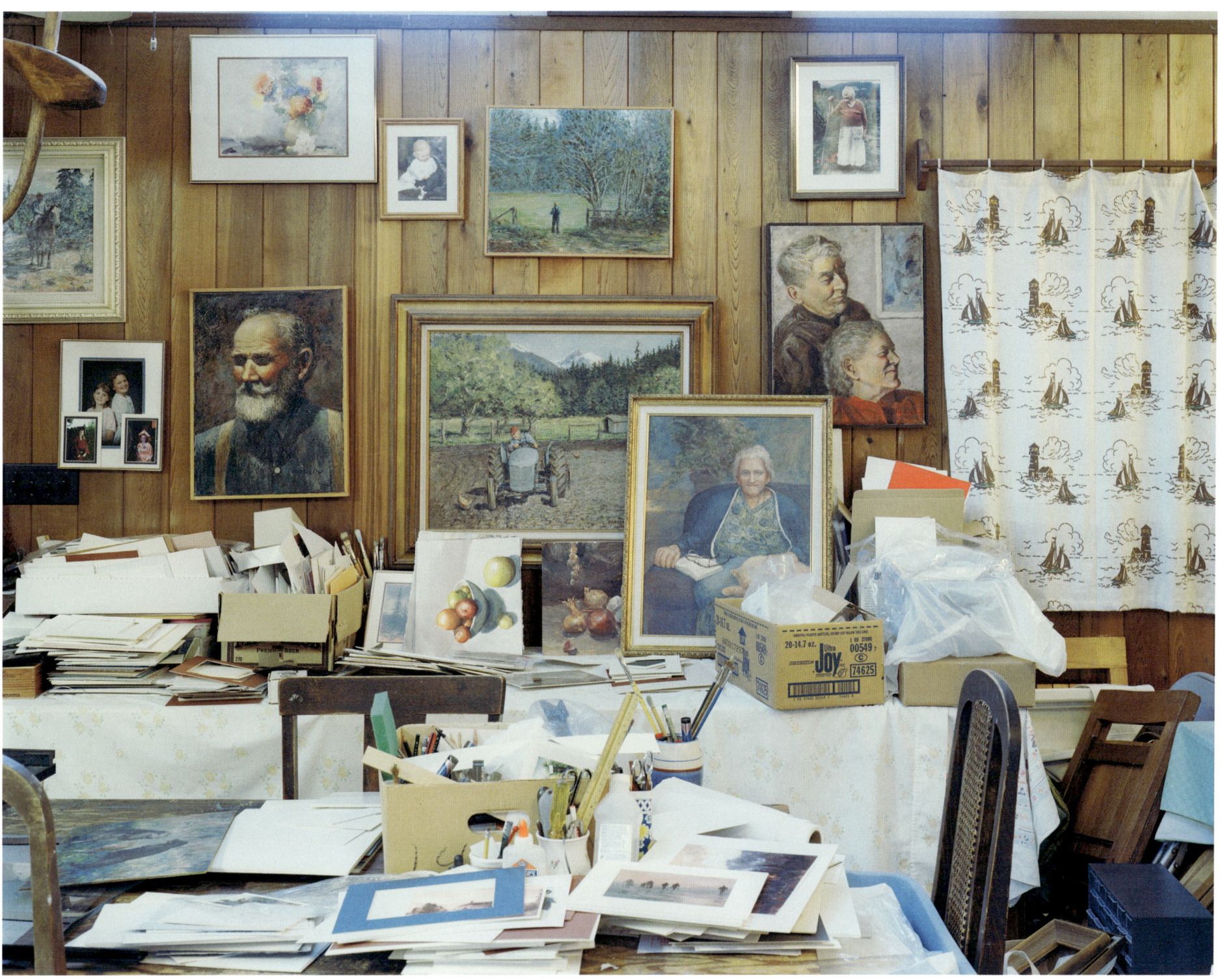

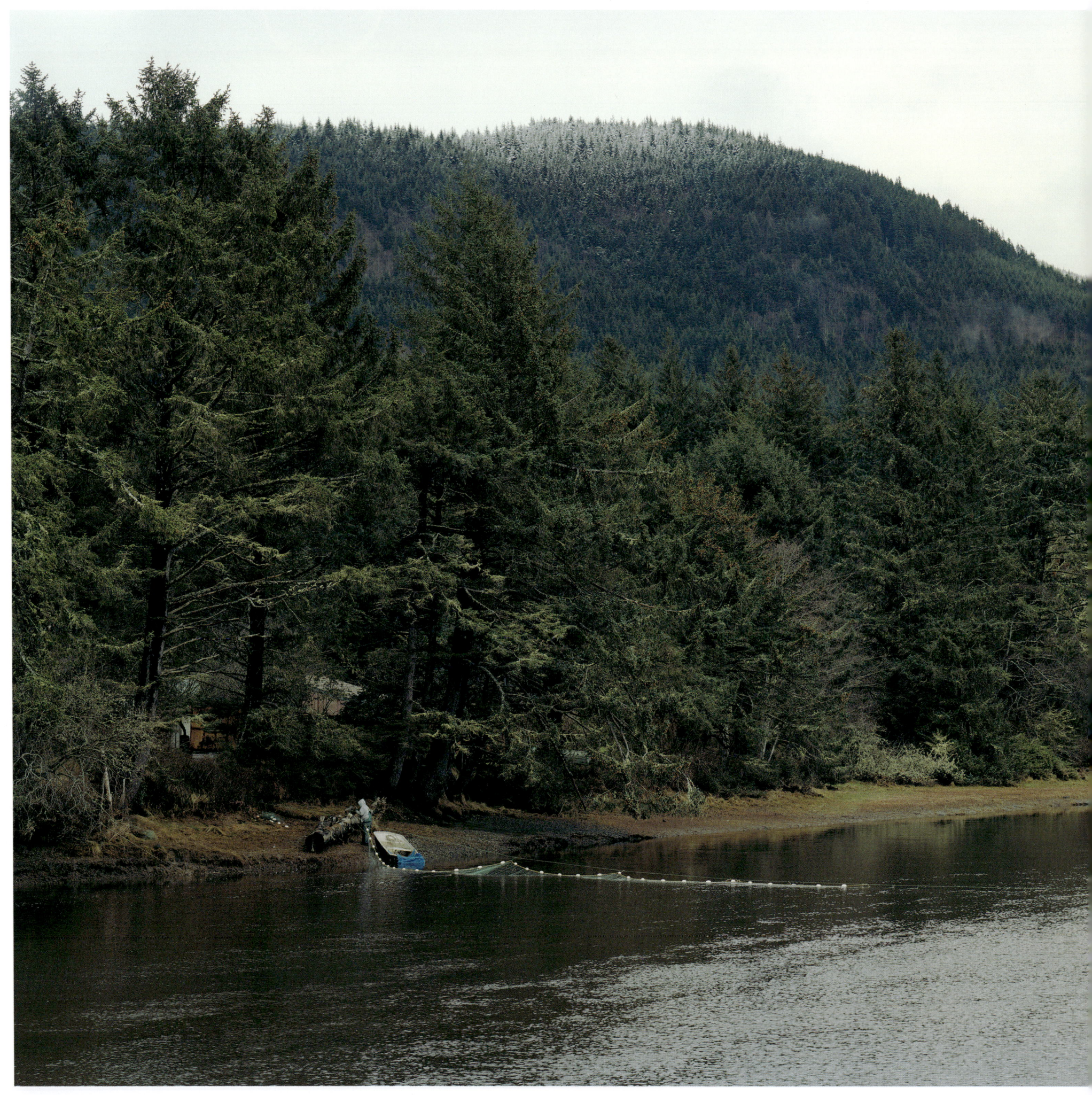

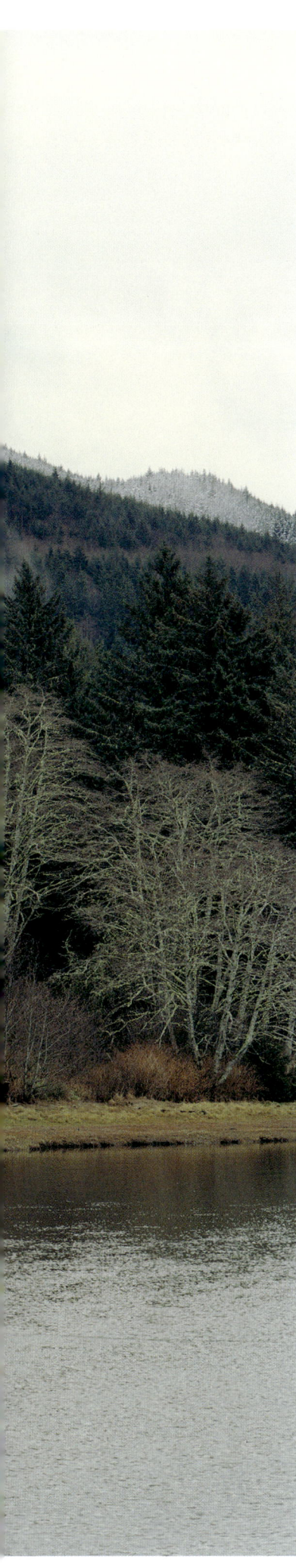

Makah tribal gill nets on the Sooes River outside Neah Bay, Washington 109

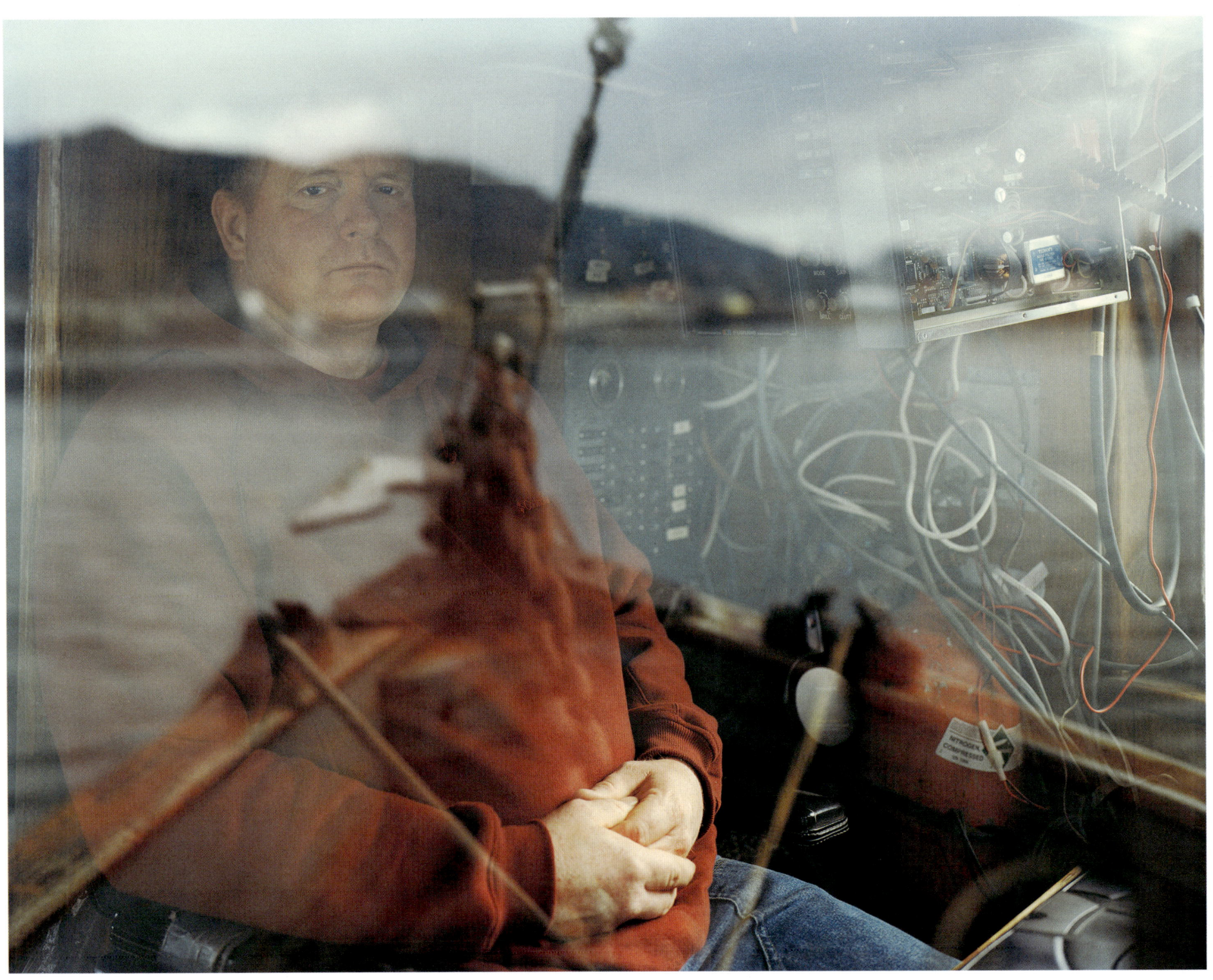

110   Brad Balderson on his longliner, the *Fish Hog*, Neah Bay, Washington

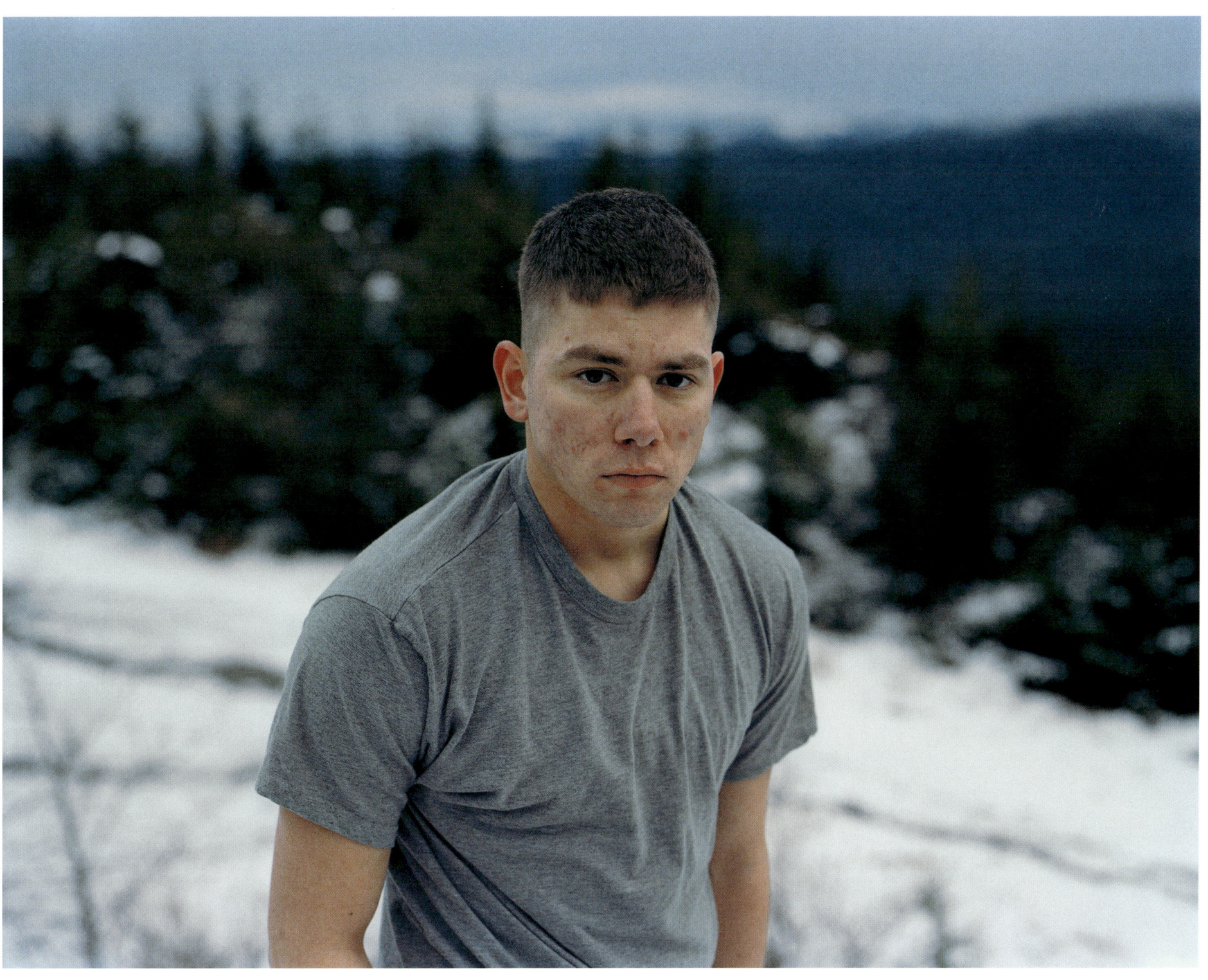

Harold Balderson, Neah Bay, Washington   111

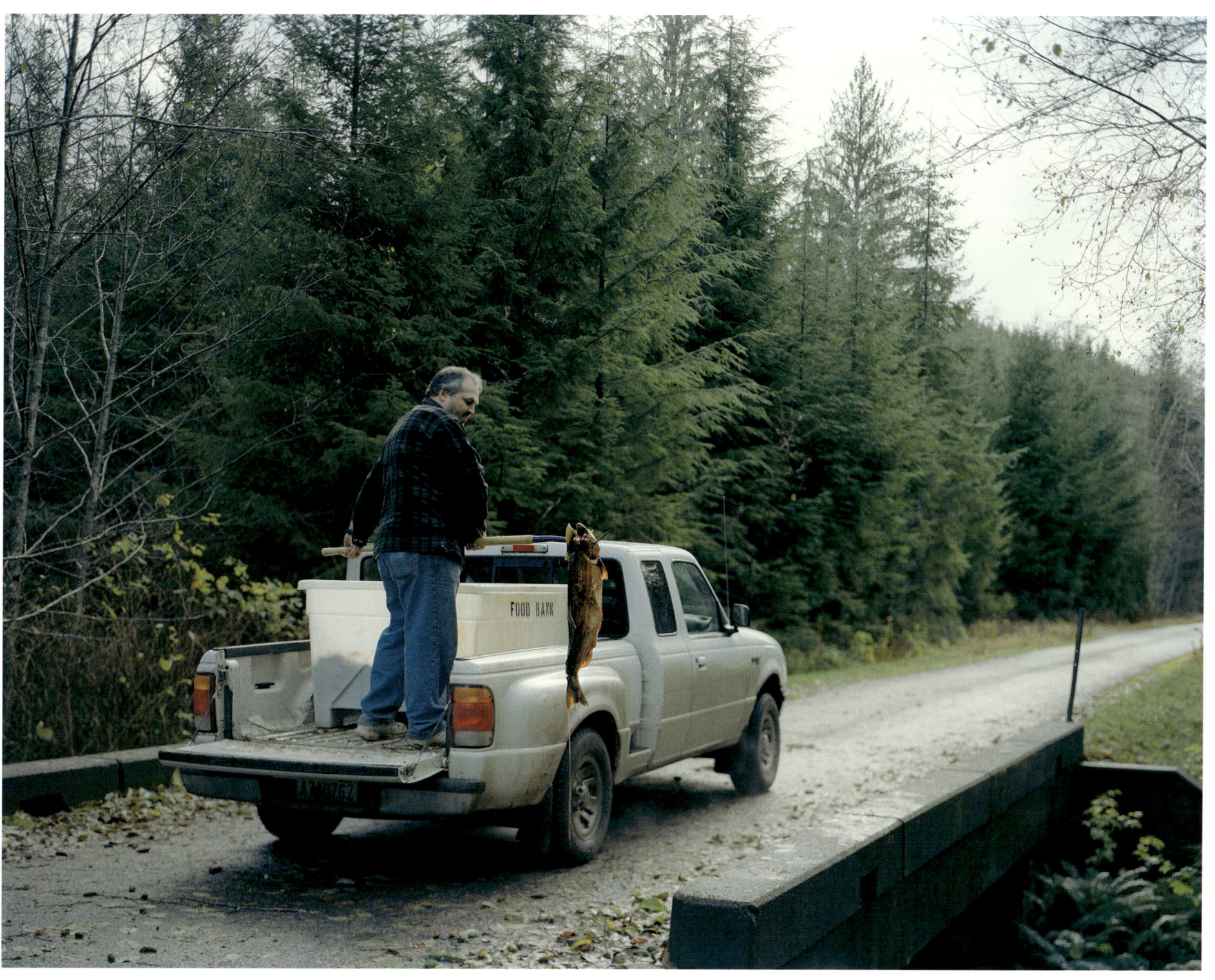

Carl placing hatchery salmon carcasses in stream near Sappho, Washington   113

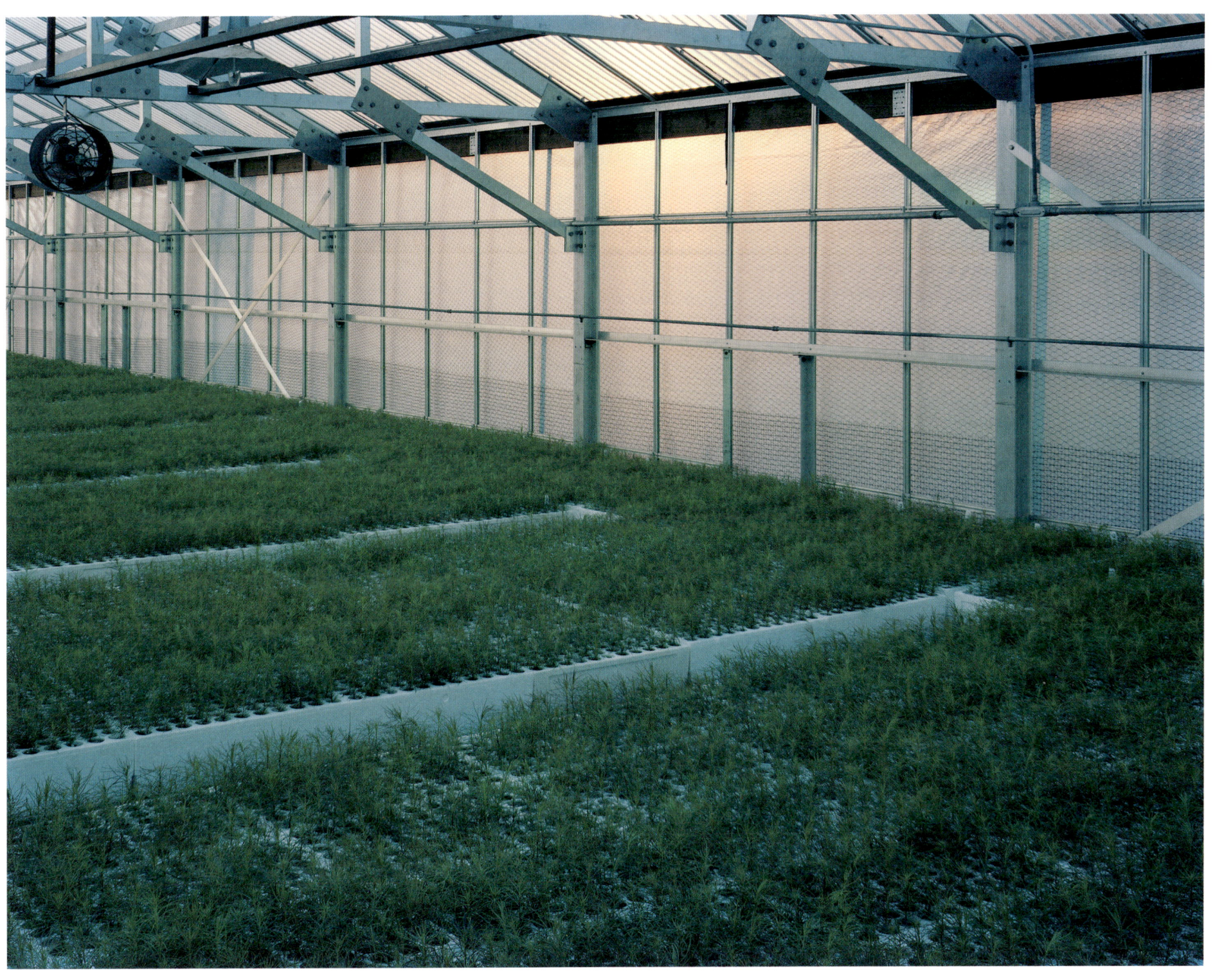

Western larch seedlings, Webster Forest Nursery, Tumwater, Washington   115

116   José planting Douglas fir seedlings outside Rainier, Oregon

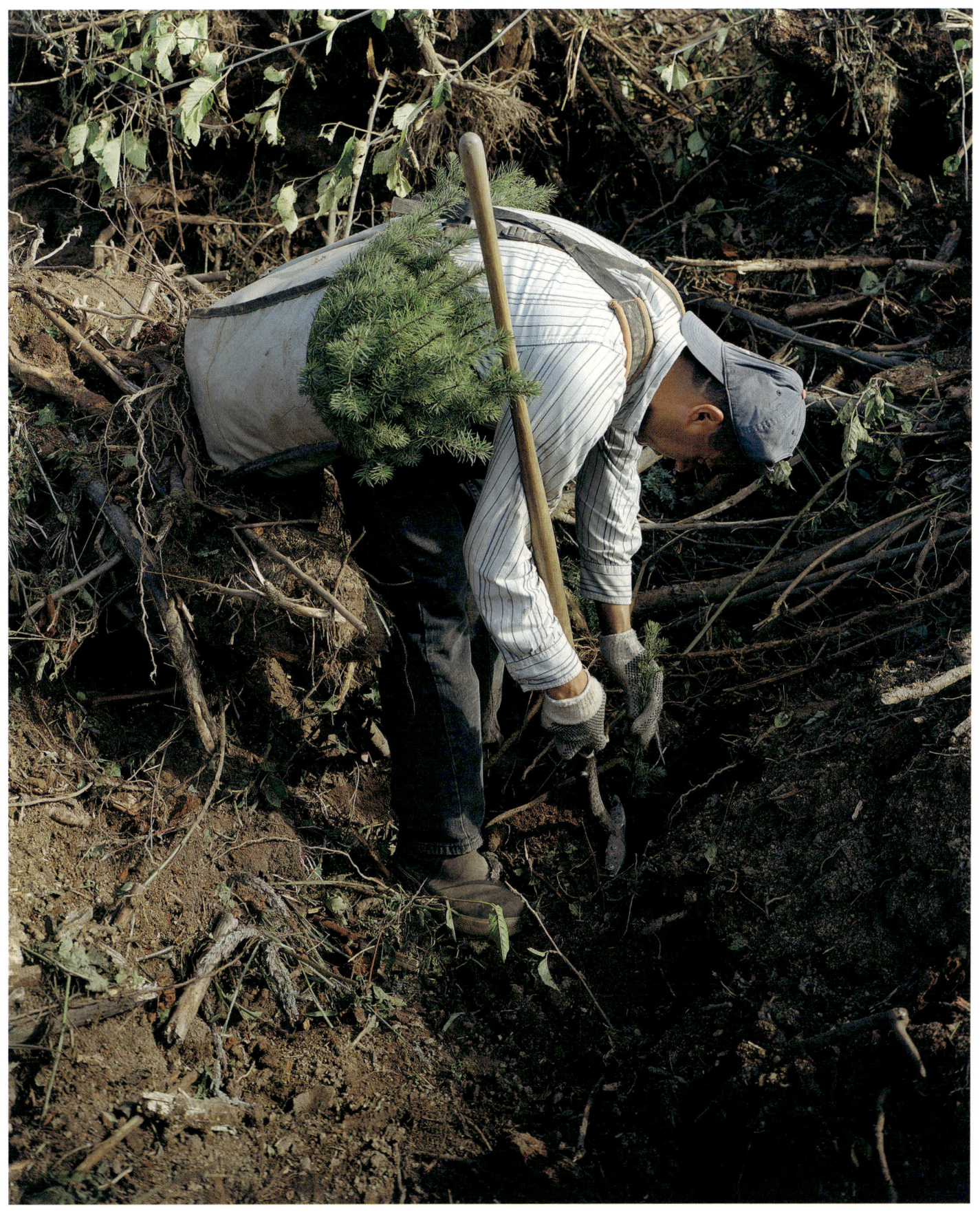

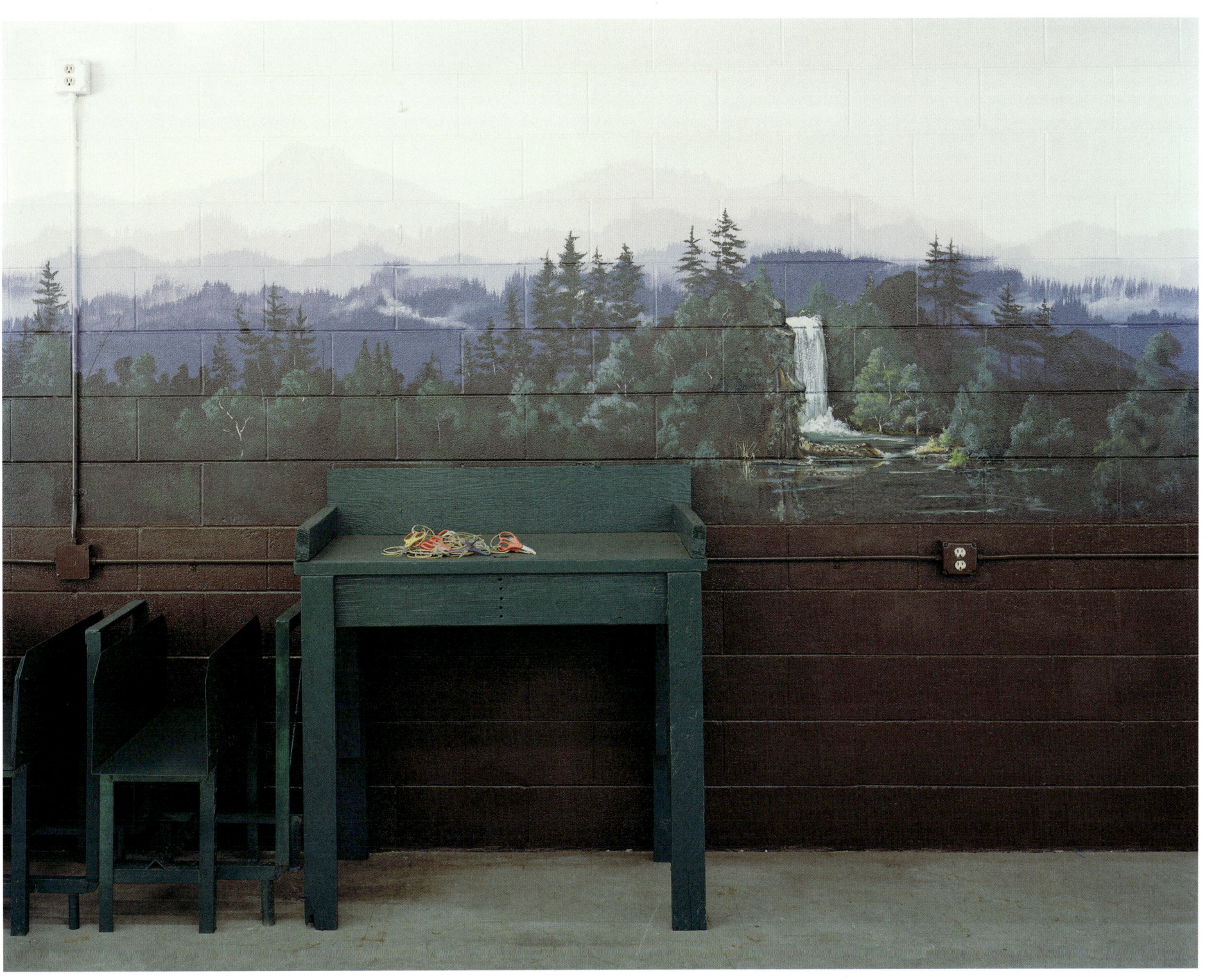

Seedling packing facility, Webster Forest Nursery, Tumwater, Washington   119

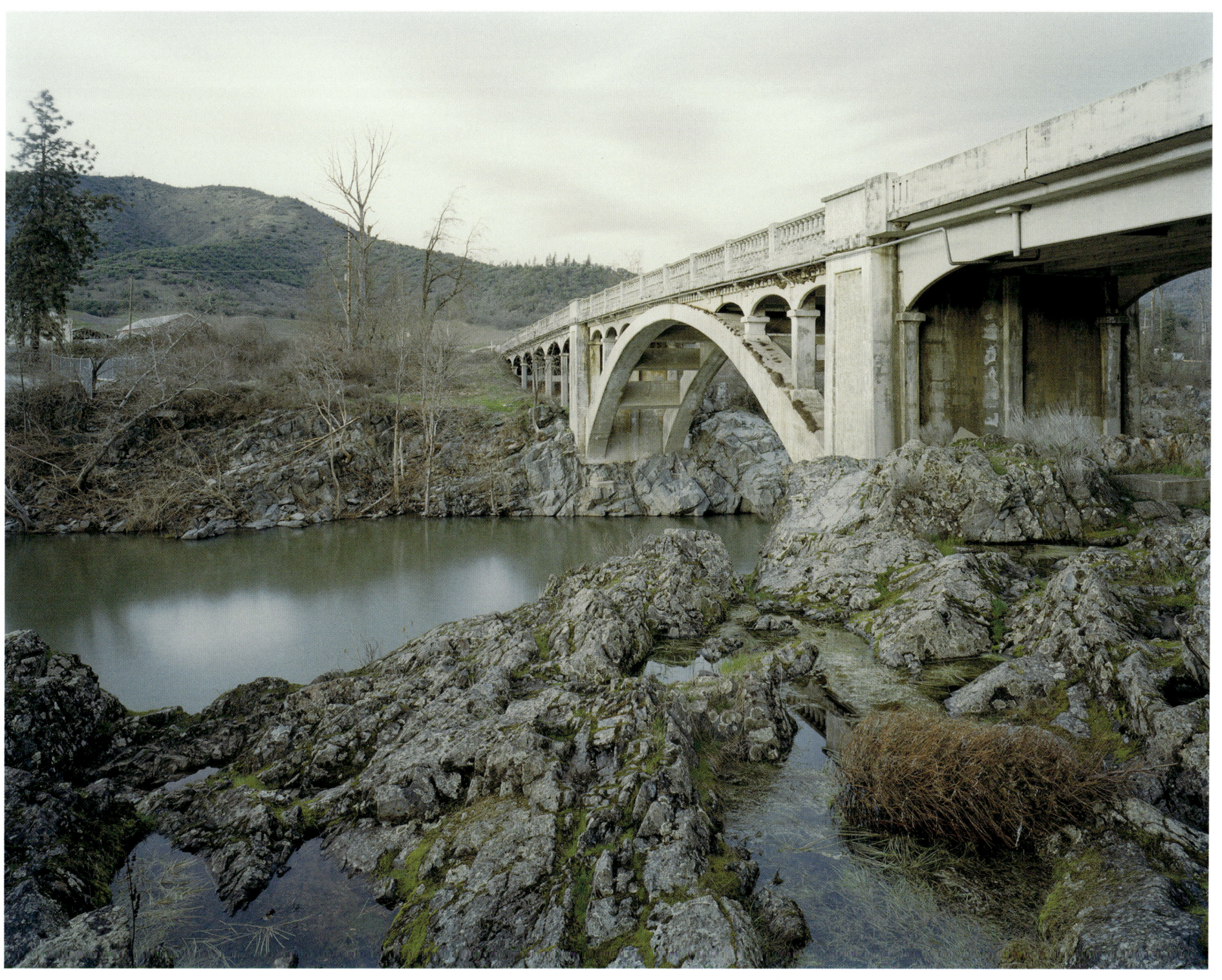

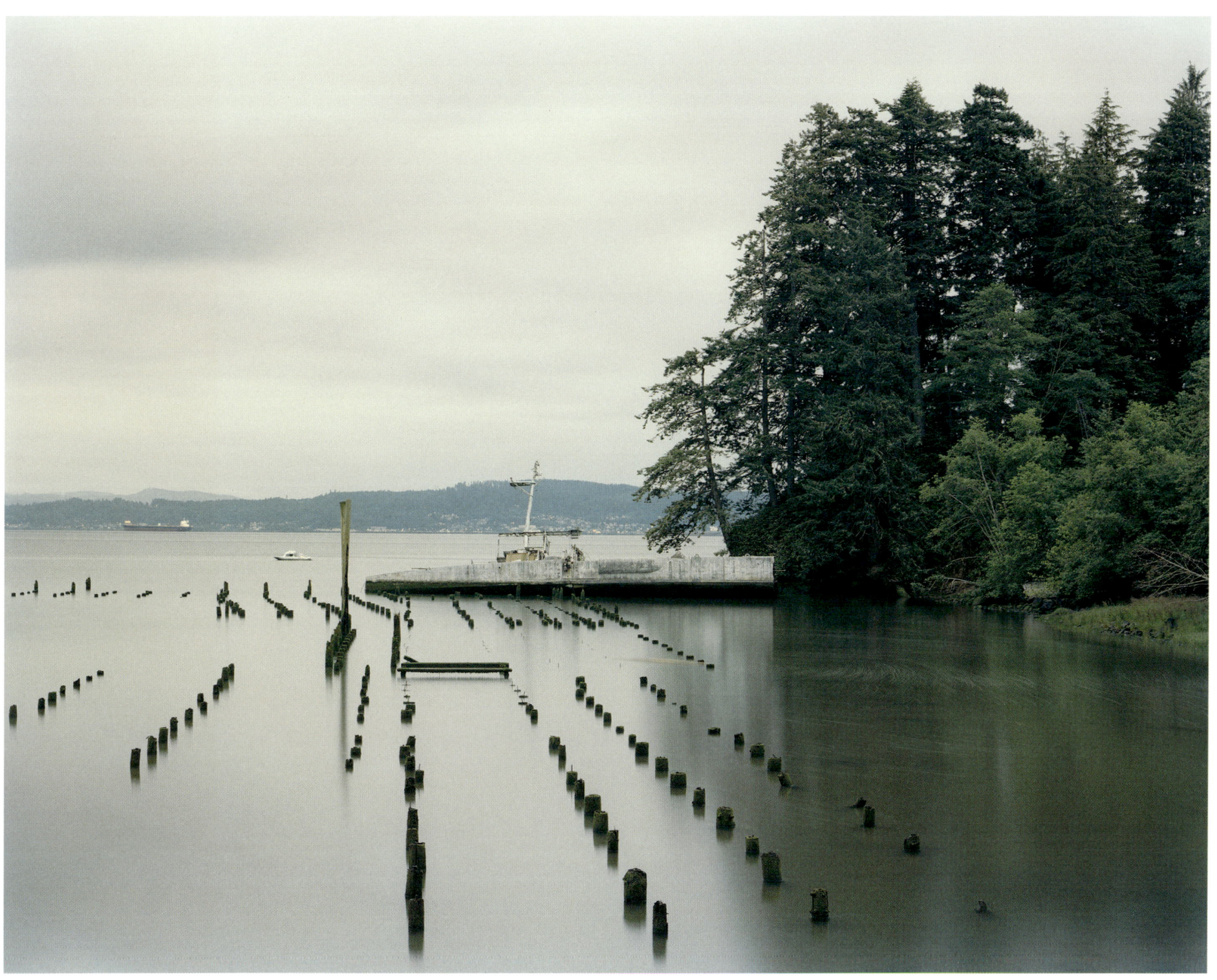

Shipwreck and salmon fishermen on the Columbia River between Washington and Oregon   *123*

124   Destruction Island, off the coast of Washington

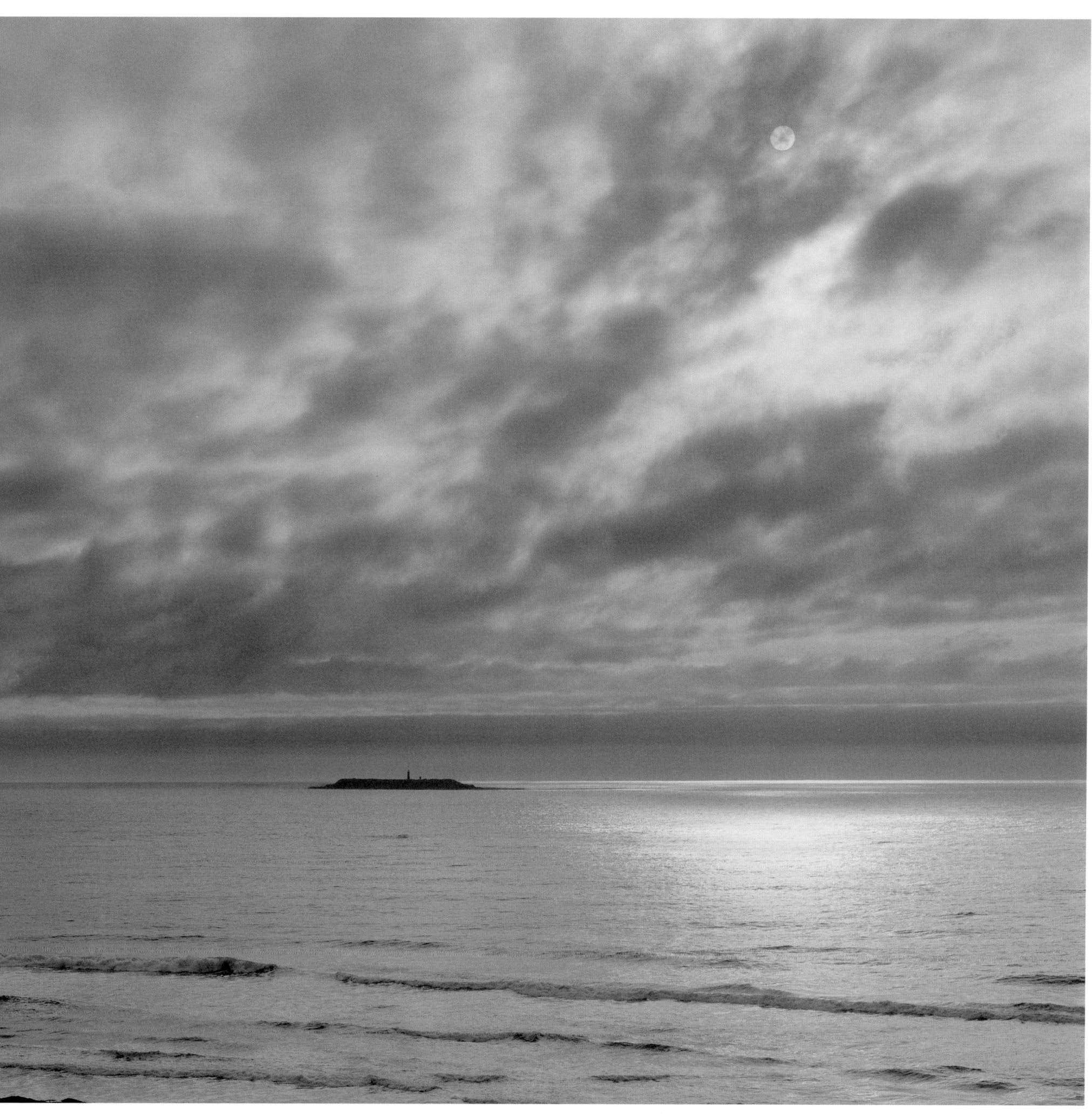

AFTER THE CHAINSAWS:
THE ALCHEMY OF RESTORATION

Tess Gallagher

Sawdust and pitch—these two scents bind me inextricably to the logging days of my childhood on the Olympic Peninsula in Washington State. Sawdust from my father's chainsaw sprayed out like a particulate blood-sign of tree-flesh. Chainsaw noise ripped through the greater silence of the forest. Trees, I felt sure at the time, never meant to speak so nakedly aloud in what, as a child, I took for pain. Nor, in their lashing down, had I ever seen anything so violent as their boughs whipping and thrashing the earth in frenzy.

Sawdust filtered down my neck into my clothes, into the cuffs of my father's trousers, caught in my mother's jet-black braids, wound to the back of her head. Pitch-stain blotched the palms of our hands where we touched the bark and it seemed the trees had written something on our bodies we could not easily erase.

On Lost Mountain and Blue Mountain near Port Angeles I worked with my parents as they tried to wrest a living for their family from "the woods," as my father called them. My mother, who'd grown up in the Missouri Ozarks, had at thirty-three become a choker-setter in my father's independent logging outfit. She needed the sure-footedness of an acrobat to walk the trunk of a tree with its limbs splaying out and the tree twitching, full of death-life against the ground. She had to drag a thick steel cable behind her and to snaffle it around the felled tree. Then it could be yarded by that cable into the "landing" and sawed into pulpwood, or the tree would be delimbed and winched whole onto the truck bed for transport to the lumber mill.

Before her marriage, my mother had been a one-room schoolteacher in Missouri, then a cook and maid to wealthy people in Denver. But in the Northwest she did a man's work, for very few women worked at logging. My parents could afford only one pair of caulk boots with nails in the soles, used by my father to climb and rig the spar tree. Mother walked the trees in street shoes, doubling the danger.

I was four when they gave me a measuring stick and a hatchet with which to notch markings into the tree for sawing it up into pulpwood lengths. I still remember the two strokes I made with the axe blade to remove each wedge of bark and fix a bright eyelet into the tree. I realize now that in those days there was no such thing as "childhood" in the preserved sense we know it today. Children existed much more as an extension of the needs of the family. Playtime was stolen time.

When a tree came down there would be cries from my father to "look out" and "get back!" The breaking off of the tree from its stump made a heart-wrenching noise that tore through the mountain air and seemed to accuse us. A strong feeling of indebtedness began to accumulate in me from that time, a sense of owing something back to the forests for what was taken in those needful days.

The images of that time were of my parents rolling logs with steel-pronged peeves, of my father with his axe handle swinging from his belt 115 or more feet up the spar, light shafting down through the hemlock, fir, and alder. In our family album there are no nostalgic photographs, as in the early pioneer days, of people posing near a gigantic tree just to admire the girth and stature of an upright tree. Instead there are photographs of both my father and my mother perched atop gigantic logs on the logging truck.

The ferocious power of the trees, the vivid sense that a person could easily have died out there was with me from an early age. In particular I remember my father's distraught cry to my mother once when a tree began to fall in an unanticipated direction, heading straight for my brother and me: "Get 'em! Get 'em! Get 'em!" and mother swooping down on us with force and shoving us into a ditch, the whoosh and crash of boughs and trunk above us, mother's body pressed to us and the light blotted out. Afterward, my father's fear gave over to relief so quickly, he spent a good while swearing at us.

Given this implicit danger and uncertainty, our parents, who contended with trees, did not seem human-sized, but in some heroic realm when compared to the parents of my playmates who worked in shops or on farms. I recall once having wandered off and getting myself lost from the logging clearing, then realizing what the trees were like all to themselves when no human was there. I felt calm and peaceful with them, but also glad when my parents' cries of "over here!" brought me back to them. How precious we all became as a family to each other during those days when we were just making a living.

These were the early 1950s, the period when sawdust really began to fly, when crosscut saws and horses were retired. I do still recall the horse my father used in his earliest days of logging. His name was Dick, and once my father's logging partner, Ownie Brown, discovered that Dick had wandered into his house and demolished an ironing board and the baby's cradle. There was something forlorn about Dick, as if his release from harness signaled the clear-cut era when a logging site began to resemble a war zone, encrusted with rubble of slash and stumps, with often nothing left standing except a few wispy saplings of no account or the lone spar itself.

Port Angeles was a pulp-mill town and when my father hadn't money to lease land for logging he would work a stint at one of two mills. He hated that work and would come home caked in the yellow sulfur used in the pulping process. The sulfur turned his pocket money black, but it still bought our school lunches.

Once my schoolmates and I toured the mill nearest our house on Caroline Street and stared into the enormous open vat where the trees, assaulted by chemicals, became a kind of soup, before being turned into paper. Each of us was given some raw pulp out of which we made a small swatch of paper. I have never forgotten this marvel. I wrote my name on the brown-pebbled surface when it had dried. I think perhaps my poetry was born somehow out of the crucible of trees falling, then being reconstituted as paper onto which words could reach again into silence and starlight and rain falling onto boughs. Indeed, I never write a word on paper without thinking of the trees out of which it is made.

By the time the disappearing spotted owl had driven logging onto private land in the mid-eighties, I had formed a pattern of traveling back East to teach at various universities, then coming home each summer to the Northwest. I have never been able to do without the moss-light brooding of my birthplace. There seems a quality of thought in this part of the country that I depend on for my poems and sense of well-being.

I have traveled the world enough to know that, despite all that has been done to the forests and waters here, this hard-to-convey turn of mind, which allows the imagination to both inhabit and to range out into the cosmos unimpeded, still exists and nourishes me and others who find their way here. "My thoughts went out of the world/To somewhere utterly alone" writes Wang Wei (701–761), Chinese poet of the Tang Dynasty. This going-out-of-the-world seems essential to the way I make poems, and I first experienced this in the forests of the Northwest.

The forest was both my playmate and my place of young self-proving, but it was also where I witnessed the helpless plundering my parents carried out at their daily peril. I identified in a very complex way, both with the trees and with my parents, as I lived the urgencies of our survival.

I admired my parents' stamina and courage, felt proud of them in the way of those who have witnessed enormous feats of strength. Yet the experience also carried sadness beyond my grasp as a child. What lingered was having found that great opening, by way of the forest presence, into recognitions beyond language. The forests, even though clear-cut, still seem to inhabit my imagination in a way that spires up in me to this day. They are alive beyond the damages and vanishing they sustained during that time of pioneer ignorance when a forest was thought to be endlessly renewable, something simply to be made use of. I recall hating the word *harvest* as applied to logging, for I instinctively thought it untrue to the nature of a forest, a term misapplied by those with the power and will to overwhelm any notion that forests could disappear, or that they had intrinsic qualities necessary to the human spirit.

Early on I formed the ambition to touch the world back with the beauty of trees and the dark silence of forests. I hoped to draw the mind out of the merely human with images of the forest in my poems such as "the angel wings of the hemlocks." I also hoped that even one verse might give pause to those Sunday loggers cutting trees with chainsaws in their backyards. But I was equally implicated in the mania for gaining "a better view." One day, I decided I wanted to see snow on the mountain, and went out to cut a sapling that was in the way. But before I could do anything I glimpsed a bird's nest high up in that tree. Then I wrote:

> *Suddenly, in every tree,*
> *an unseen nest*
> *where a mountain*
> *would be.*

We are always prioritizing: the eagle over the raven, the spotted owl over the barred owl, fishing and water rights over the health of salmon runs, the view of the mountains over the view of the trees; I wanted to turn the tables on our notion of what "a view" requires. Maybe we needed another kind of seeing altogether. And this is what the Northwest still offers, an alchemy of seeing—the notion of earth, of forest and sea, as embodiments speaking to us with their very essence, yet also existing beyond us and not for our purposes alone.

As someone who returned to her disheveled birthplace, I have had to experience this still-beautiful land in the dirge of what was ruined and ransacked of our forests, land, and water. I recall the first time I came home from the East Coast and drove toward the ocean, seeing to my left the vast clear-cuts that still exist, and to my right the Strait of Juan de Fuca and finally, the ocean. I realized then that things had gotten terribly out of hand.

But due to a slow, steady turn away from destructive practices and attitudes that brought us to this dismay, I believe the Northwest's natural gifts are going to be more fully cherished. The choices toward selective logging, restoring wild runs of salmon, protecting wetlands and watersheds, and setting our priorities for other than simply economic reasons will hopefully become the expected way we do things here.

I have thankfully lived long enough to be able to witness a turn, in which the various industries at work do not hold all the cards. Ordinary citizens have now gained an awareness that allows them to do amazing things, like take down the Elwha dams in the hopes of restoring the wild salmon runs to this glacier-fed river. Nearby in the Dungeness

Valley the rampant retirement developments under the "rain shadow" have been given pause by land trusts, which preserve farms and save meadows and grazing zones.

We have also come into a more respectful awakening to the Native American presence here through the discovery, in 2003, of an ancient village called Tse-whit-zen (pronounced ch-WHEET-son), which existed for over 2,700 years, from 750 B.C. The village, buried for over a hundred years, was discovered along Port Angeles Harbor during a project to build pontoons for the Hood Canal Bridge. The Lower Elwha Klallam Tribe hopes to build a museum on the spot where many graves were disturbed and important artifacts discovered. This is one of the most exciting "finds" in our state and once established will allow the ancient presence of Native Americans here to become a more central element of our consciousness, whereas during my upbringing it really was hardly acknowledged.

Despite this positive turn in awareness that favors vigilance in protecting our legacy and our environment, a panic often attends our reaching toward restorative measures. We feel overwhelmed, as if it is too late, as if the harm may be too deep, even irredeemable. Yet to think so is self-defeating. We need the images of beauty and damage and all the states in between in order to continue to enlarge our consciousness of what is happening here. My own imagination was forged in a time when I was sheltered in a cathedral of cedar stumps, and these remnants still haunt and dwarf me.

As a child I used to help my father clean fish on the grass of our backyard. I recall touching the tightly packed orange beads of salmon eggs held in an invisible slick of membrane. The silky miracle of that touch stays in my hand, just as the sunlight rainbowing on the silver salmon's scales seemed to brand my consciousness with the ocean-light from which it came. There is a deep sadness I still carry for the loss of the forests, as I knew them, and for the fish that are no longer present in such bounty as they were in the 1950s, and before that, in the times of the Native American tribes who lived by fishing and hunting.

But possibility is returning—the possibility of mind that the forests and the gunmetal gray waters here allow—not only to poets, but perhaps to all, that presence by which we may give way to elements other than ourselves.

In the way of modern efficiencies, the sawdust that whipped across my childhood path is no longer simply a waste product, but reappears now as wood pellets for fuel. In fact, I am told, there is now effectively no such thing as waste-wood in the lumber industry. Of course, a forest's ecology thrives as much on what is rotting as on what is growing, so it is curious to think of an immaculate way of taking the trees from the forest so no sign of what occurred remains.

The pulp mill where my father filled his lungs with sulfur fumes closed in 2000, but the clean up of the toxins is ongoing nine years after. A tourist facility is proposed for the site. I have sold the boat in which my late husband, Raymond Carver, and I used to fish for salmon in the Straits. His fishing rod is on loan to an enthusiast in Seattle while my own stands in permanent retirement in the entry to our house. There just aren't enough fish in the current runs to make me feel buoyant toward a fishing trip.

Yet being in the Northwest during this present time is, for me, more about intangible images—like staring into seawater scalded with sunlight and thinking of fish alive, unseen somewhere below. Such experiences cause an inner spaciousness into which we can be submerged for a few moments, and then renewed by unseen elements. In this manner, the forests I carried from childhood in my imagination and the ocean-floating mind I discovered while fishing with my father in the Northwest still sustain me. They shore up my entrustment to the bounty of this place and underwrite a vision that is more and more becoming shared, cherished, and protected by those around me.

Tess Gallagher is the author of fifteen books of poetry and short fiction, including the forthcoming collection, *The Man from Kinvara: Selected Stories*.

NOTES ON SELECT PHOTOGRAPHS

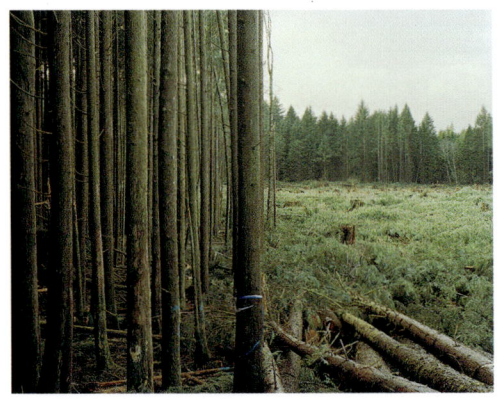

Freshly Felled Trees, Nemah, Washington
I passed by this stand of trees early in the morning, just as a crew of loggers was arriving. By dusk a long swath of the forest had been felled. Collectively, ninety percent of the coastal old-growth forests of Washington, Oregon, and California have been logged. Giant spruce, cedar, hemlock, and fir have been replaced by younger second-growth plantations of trees identical in species and age. These new "working forests," often referred to as "crops," are bred for efficiency and shorter rotations between planting and harvest. The faster trees grow, the quicker they can be harvested and a new crop planted.

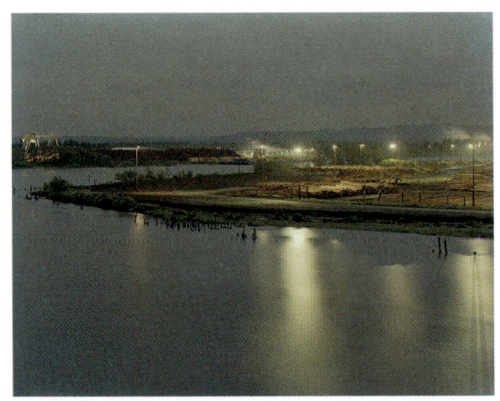

Weyerhaeuser sorting yard along the Chehalis River, Cosmopolis, Washington
Logs from throughout the Olympic Peninsula are loaded onto trucks and barges at Weyerhaeuser's "Bay City" sort yard along the Chehalis River. Further upriver sits the company's closed pulp mill where until 2006 thousands of logs were once turned into chemical pulp destined to become everything from toothbrush handles to cigarette filters and photographic paper. The mill had employed over three hundred local workers. While Weyerhaeuser remains one of the largest forest products companies in the world, corporate restructuring and expanded global operations in eighteen countries has meant the closure of numerous mills throughout the Northwest.

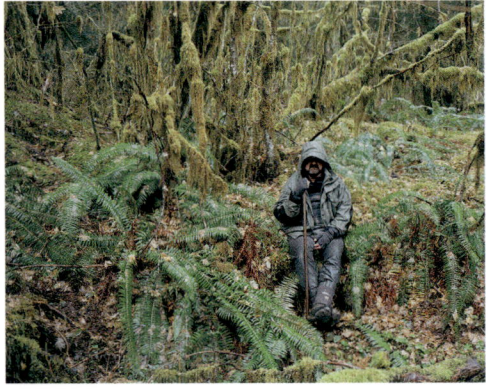

Roger Mosley counting Coho spawn nests along the upper Sol Duc River, Washington
I spent a very wet November day with Roger Mosley, hiking through dense forest and forging small tributaries of the Sol Duc River. Roger works for Washington State's Department of Fish and Wildlife, locating and counting salmon ("reds") nests buried in sandy riverbeds where spawning Coho and Chinook salmon deposit their eggs. On our hike, Roger and I found only a handful of reds along with a few Coho, their bodies crimson and scarred from fighting their way to spawning grounds upstream. Weeks of heavy rain meant the river was too muddy for most salmon to navigate.

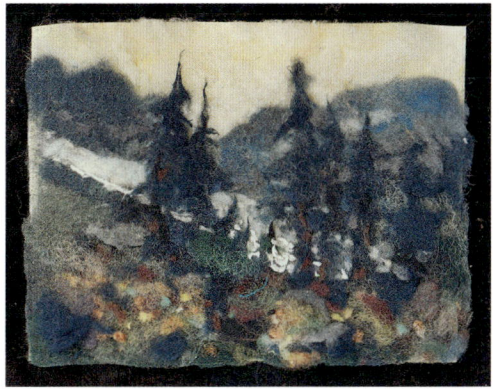

Missy Barlow's dryer lint landscape, lower Hoh River, Washington

Elizabeth "Missy" Barlow has lived most of her eighty-seven years on Washington State's Olympic Peninsula, along the remote lower Hoh River, just before it empties into the Pacific Ocean. Her grandfather, one of the first white settlers to the region, homesteaded nearby land after making his way West following the Civil War. Both a trained botanist and artist, Missy has a jar full of blue ribbons won at regional art competitions for her oils and watercolors, and for her unique lint "paintings." Over the years, friends and family have sent Missy their own dryer lint, expanding her palette of colors and textures beyond what her own wardrobe provides. The muted tones of her lint creations befit the rain-soaked hillsides surrounding Missy's home.

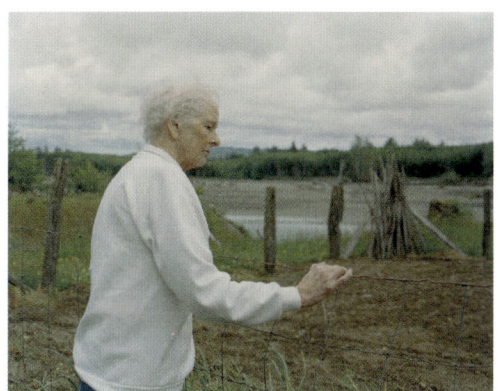

Missy by her garden, lower Hoh River, Washington

Once a botany student at the University of Washington, Missy spent years creating a new hybrid variety of potato. Leading me out to a freshly tilled field on the banks of the Hoh River, Missy recounted how she had crossed a purple potato given to her by her aunt with a native *ozette* or "Indian potato." The new variety was aptly named "Missy's Purple Cross" and combined the best properties of both its indigenous and conventional parents.

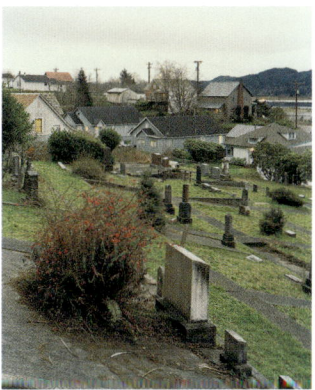

Gardiner, Oregon

When his schooner ran aground on the Umpqua River banks in 1850, Boston merchant Gardiner Chism simply brought his cargo ashore and built a town. The town quickly grew into an important lumber and shipping port. In the 1960s, International Paper built a large mill in Gardiner, employing hundreds from the region. The mill was demolished in 2006 and the site is currently for sale.

Elwha River Dam, Washington

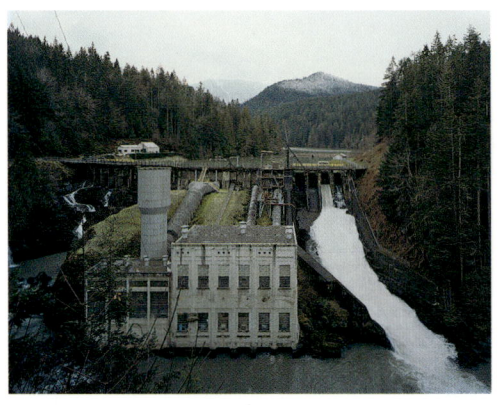

The 108-foot-tall Elwha River Dam was built on the Olympic Peninsula in the early 1900s to provide power for the local paper mill. Originally built in violation of state law requiring passage for fish, the Elwha Dam, along with the Glines Canyon Dam further upriver, prevents nearly a half-million salmon and steelhead from reaching what had been one of the most productive river ecosystems in the continental United States. In response to pressure by a coalition of conservation groups, Native American tribal councils, fishermen, and politicians, the Federal Government will begin work removing both of the outdated dams in 2012. The project will cost nearly $200 million and take years to complete, but eventually seventy miles of spawning habitat will be reclaimed, and biologists believe that the fish will return.

Cindy, Nemah River Hatchery, Washington

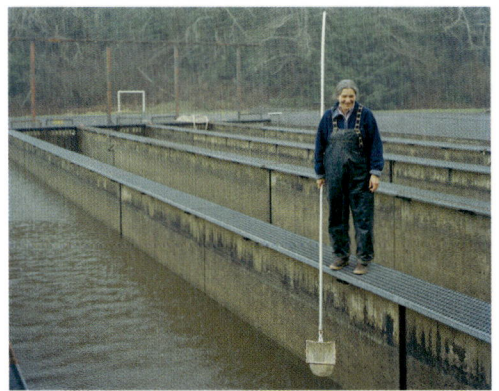

For nearly twenty years Cindy Millage has worked for hatcheries run by the state's Department of Fish and Wildlife. She's spent the last six years managing the Nemah River Hatchery, raising two and a half million Chinook, a half million Coho, and thousands of chum, all of which supplement the dwindling stocks of wild salmon. Over the years Cindy has hiked every trail within the Olympic National Park and Forest, hiking most trails alone. "My first solo backpack in the Olympics was when I was twenty years old. I crossed from the Queets River over to the Quinault via the abandoned Tshletshy Creek Trail, then I hiked out the Elwha River Trail, and hitchhiked to Seattle. There are still places I'd like to go, but I'm slowing down."

Juan Abalos, salvaging cedar shingle bolts, lower Hoh River, Washington

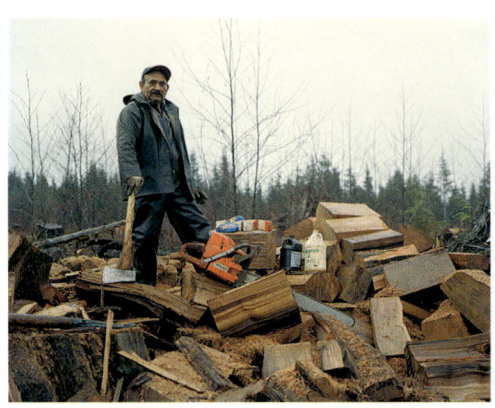

As I left Missy Barlow's home on the remote Oil City Road, I met three Mexican immigrants salvaging blocks of lumber from old cedar stumps in a swampy clearing logged long ago. Whatever good cedar was found would be sold to mills and used for roofing shingles. Juan Abalos, came from the state of Michoacan and had been working in the U.S. for the past twenty-five years. With him was Heriberto, who came from Jalisco six years ago and has never made the expensive weeklong journey home, since border enforcement has grown stricter. Immigrant workers make up a growing percentage of the region's rural workforce, planting seedlings, harvesting wild mushrooms and floral greens, shucking oysters, and processing fish.

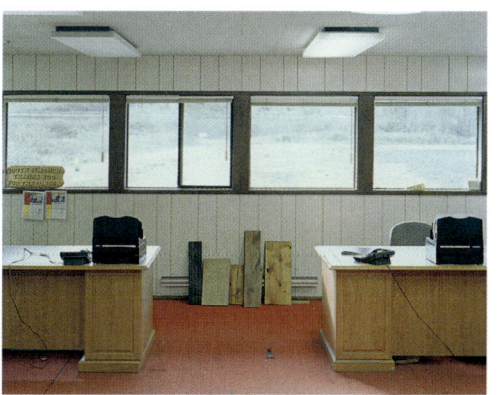

Offices, Seaport Lumber, South Bend, Washington

Mark Murphy and his two partners started Seaport Lumber three years ago in South Bend, Washington, after the mill's previous owner had gone bankrupt. The mill had been put up for long-term lease by the county with the provision that any new owner keep the mill operational. Pacific County has one of the highest unemployment rates in the state and the mill had been a good source of employment. Seaport Lumber now does a big business in milling Alder. Once considered a "weed" by the timber industry, there is now huge demand for Alder wood, a favorite of furniture and laminates factories.

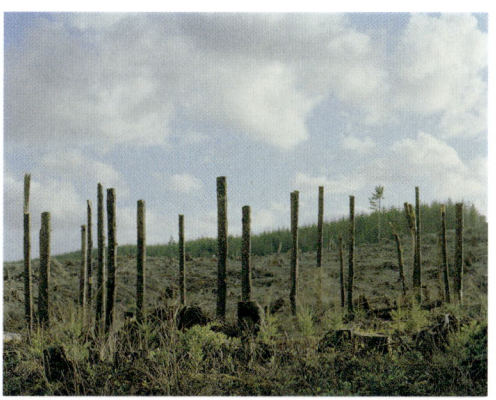

Topped trees reserved for wildlife, Nemah, Washington

A sad-looking band of young trees, their branches and tops removed, lines a stretch of recently logged land near the Nemah River. These trees were most likely left by the logging crew as "snags" for wildlife habitat. Snags are typically dead or dying trees that provide shelter and food for hundreds of cavity-nesting birds and mammals. While leaving a small stand of topped trees along the edge of a clear-cut might meet the state's requirements for snag preservation or creation, it is no replacement for a diverse and healthy ecosystem.

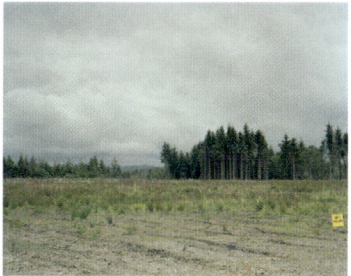 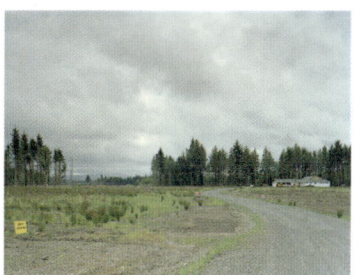

Willapa Sands Estates, South Bend, Washington

Increasingly, Weyerhaeuser and other forest-products companies have moved into the real estate business. Once a forest is harvested, subsidiary companies sell the land for development, earning money off the trees and money off the land. It is a practice known as "log it and flog it." The forty-acre gated community of Willapa Sands Estates is currently under construction on Washington's southwestern coast. Promotional materials boast that, "Dreams do come true! Bay frontage such as this doesn't come along everyday and this luxury is getting scarce. Come pick your lot."

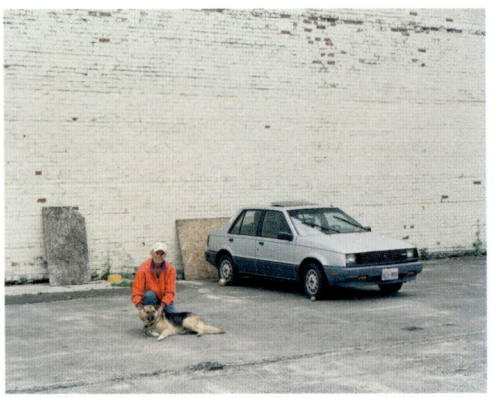

Jim and Star, Aberdeen, Washington
Jim works as a handyman for Mac's tavern and some of the other businesses in town. When we met, his German shephard, Star, was sitting in the shade next to Jim's car. "Star's been stolen a few times when I'm inside working," Jim told me. "I always get 'im back though." A padlock now dangles from Star's collar.

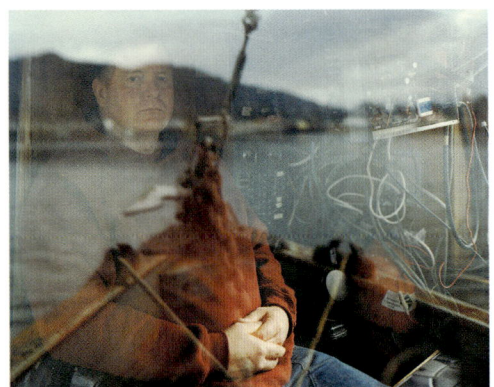

Brad Balderson on his longliner, the *Fish Hog*, Neah Bay, Washington
Brad Balderson has been a commercial fisherman in the Makah tribal reservation town of Neah Bay for more than twenty years. When I visited in January, Brad's boat the *Fish Hog* was set up for longlining black cod and he was hoping to make the forty-mile journey off shore as soon as the weather broke. Depending on the season, Brad also fishes for chinook, halibut, rockfish, and dogfish. In addition to shrinking quotas and costly licenses for each fishery, he pays increasingly more for fuel. Brad thought that he might soon sell his own boat and permits to the Federal Government as part of its buy-out program.

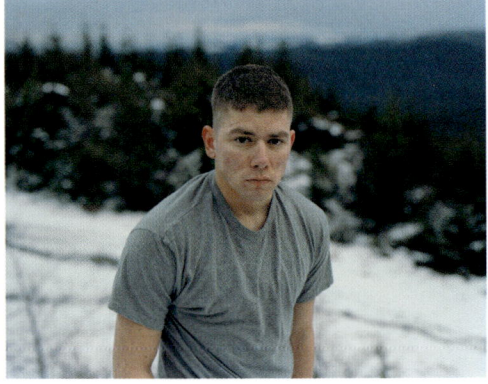

Harold Balderson, Neah Bay, Washington
The youngest of Brad Balderson's four sons, Harold had just returned home to Neah Bay from military service in Iraq. He had celebrated his twentieth birthday, building bases for the Army in a landscape far removed from his home. "I joined the Army to get out and see the world," Harold told me. Unlike his father and brothers, Harold has no interest in becoming a fisherman.

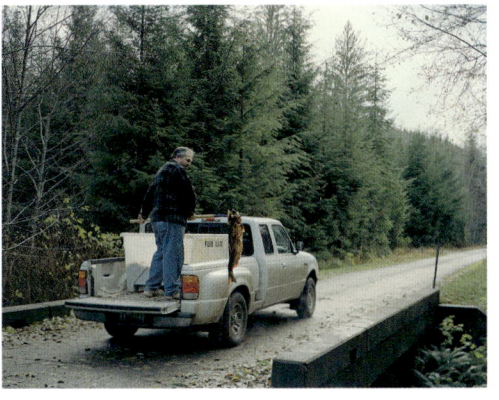

Carl placing hatchery salmon carcasses in stream near Sappho, Washington
Carl Chastain is the executive director of the Pacific Coast Salmon Coalition, a non-profit organization that helps restore salmon habitat on the Olympic Peninsula. Working together with local hatcheries, Carl and coalition volunteers collect the carcasses of thousands of spawning hatchery salmon, their eggs already gathered for the coming year. Some of the fish are taken to local food banks, but most are placed into small streams throughout the region, providing a food source rich in nitrogen, carbon, and phosphorous to wild salmon juveniles.

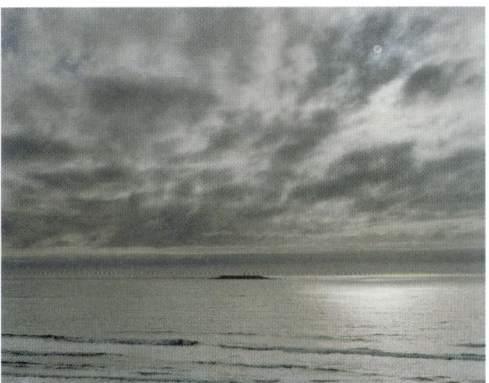

Destruction Island, off the coast of Washington
Three miles off the coast of the Olympic Peninsula sits Destruction Island, the only offshore island along Washington State's remote outer coast. So named by the eighteenth-century British explorer Captain George Vancouver, the island was the site of many shipwrecks as merchant vessels ran aground on shallow reefs in coastal fog and storms. In 1891, a fully staffed lighthouse finally brought relief to seafarers sailing between northern mill towns and San Francisco. Today the lighthouse is automated, the island reclaimed by flocks of seabirds. It stands as a symbol of the region's past, its hardscrabble identity, and the turbulent future that must now be navigated.

EIRIK JOHNSON

1974   Born in Seattle

1997   Graduates with a BFA from University of Washington in Seattle

1999   Travels to Peru on a Fulbright Grant

2003   Receives MFA from San Francisco Art Institute

2005   Publishes first monograph, *Borderlands*, and wins the Santa Fe Prize for Photography

2006   Begins teaching photography at Massachusetts College of Art and Design in Boston

SOLO EXHIBITIONS

2009   *Sawdust Mountain*, G. Gibson Gallery, Seattle; Henry Art Gallery, Seattle; Rena Bransten Gallery, San Francisco

2007   *Animal Holes*, G. Gibson Gallery, Seattle

2006   *Eirik Johnson: Borderlands*, Yossi Milo Gallery, New York

2005   *Eirik Johnson: Borderlands*, Museum of Contemporary Photography, Columbia College, Chicago

        Eirik Johnson, Rena Bransten Gallery, San Francisco

2002   *West Oakland Walk*, Diego Rivera Gallery, San Francisco

2000   *Eirik Johnson: Estonopeica y Estereoscópicas*, Ojo Ajeno Galería, Centro de la Fotografía, Lima, Peru

        Eirik Johnson: Redefining the Western Landscape, Saddleback College Art Gallery, Mission Viejo, California

        Tawantinsuyo: Un Viaje Fotográfico, Museum of Contemporary Art, Cusco, Peru

1999   *Western Ground*, RayKo South, San Francisco

1998   *Western Ground*, G. Gibson Gallery, Seattle

GROUP EXHIBITIONS

2008   *Animal Intelligence*, Project Gallery, Ann Arbor, Michigan

2007   *Utopian Mirage: Social Metaphors in Contemporary Photography and Film*, Frances Lehman Loeb Art Center, Vassar College, Poughkeepsie, New York

        On the Wall: Aperture Magazine '05/'06, Aperture Gallery, New York

2005   *Vital Signs*, George Eastman House, Rochester, New York

2004   *Boundaries*, Angie Newman Johnson Gallery, Episcopal Academy, Alexandria, Virginia

        Landscape, Rena Bransten Gallery, San Francisco

        Oculus, ASA Gallery, University of New Mexico, Albuquerque

        Residency Finalist Exhibition, Headlands Center for the Arts, Sausalito, California

2003   *Bay Area Currents*, Oakland Art Gallery, Oakland, California

        Intervals, Artist Television Access, San Francisco

        New California Masters, Works/San José, San José, California

        Stanford Art Spaces 35, Stanford University, Palo Alto, California

        Vernissage, San Francisco Art Institute Master of Fine Arts Exhibition

2002   *Lucite, Longitude and Joe Namath*, collaboration with Toban Nichols, Diego Rivera Gallery, San Francisco

           Reclaiming the Hollow, site-specific installation, San Francisco

           Repurpose, Southern Exposure, San Francisco

2001   *Re-Imaging the West: A New History*, SF Camerawork, San Francisco

1999   *Commotion*, SF Camerawork, San Francisco

1998   *Selected Contemporary Work*, Robert Koch Gallery, San Francisco

1997   *Intrusion: The Contemporary Landscape*, G. Gibson Gallery, Seattle

           The Camera Obscured, FotoCircle Gallery, Seattle

PUBLICATIONS

Johnson, Eirik, and Rod Slemmons. *Borderlands*. Santa Fe, New Mexico: Twin Palms Publisher; Chicago: Museum of Contemporary Photography, 2005.

Miller, Alicia. "Re-Imaging the West: a New History." *Camerawork: A Journal of Photographic Arts* 28 (Spring/Summer 2001): p. 4.

FELLOWSHIPS AND PRIZES

2008   Massachusetts College of Art and Design Kelner Faculty Fellowship

2005   Santa Fe Prize for Photography

2003   Brooks Award to Anderson Ranch Arts Center

           San Francisco Art Institute Artist Book Competition

2001   San Francisco Art Institute Graduate Artistic Merit Fellowship

           Grant for Artist Project, Washington State Arts Council

1999   Fulbright Grant

COLLECTIONS

Artist and Special Book Collection, University of Washington, Seattle

Centro de la Fotografía, Lima, Peru

George Eastman House, Rochester, New York

Joseph and Elaine Monsen Collection, Seattle, and La Jolla, California

Museum of Contemporary Photography, Chicago

National Fulbright Organization

National Institute of Culture, Lima, Peru

Paul Sack Collection, San Francisco

ACKNOWLEDGMENTS

Among the many individuals to thank for making this book possible, I owe a special debt of gratitude to the Balderson family, Carl Chastain, Cindy Millage, Roger Mosley, Mark Murphy, and above all Missy Barlow, who infused this project with her story and soul. Thank you also to Joanna Lehan, Inger-Lise McMillan, Lesley Martin, and Michelle Dunn for their efforts and belief in this book, and to Gail Gibson and Rena Bransten for their continued support of my work. I am also deeply grateful to Tess Gallagher and David Guterson for their thoughtful contributions. Special thanks to the Henry Art Gallery and Chief Curator Elizabeth Brown for their involvement, and to the Turner Foundation for their generous support. These photographs are for my mother and father, for a childhood spent hiking the forests and fishing the waters of the Northwest. To my wife Heidi, my unending thanks for her patience and partnership.

Front cover: Freshly felled trees, Nemah, Washington
Back cover: Elwha River Dam, Washington
Frontispiece: Stacked logs in Weyerhaeuser sort yard, Cosmopolis, Washington

Editor: Joanna Lehan
Designer: Inger-Lise McMillan
Production: Sarah Henry

The staff for this book at Aperture Foundation includes: Juan García de Oteyza, *Executive Director*; Michael Culoso, *Chief Financial Officer*; Lesley A. Martin, *Publisher, Books*; Susan Ciccotti, *Senior Text Editor, Books*; Nima Etemadi, *Editorial Assistant*; Matthew Pimm, *Production Director*; Andrea Smith, *Director of Communications*; Kristian Orozco, *Sales Director*; Diana Edkins, *Director of Exhibitions and the Paul Strand Archive*; Kellie McLaughlin, *Director of Limited-Edition Photographs*; Alex Freedman, Matt Minor, Benedikt Reichenbach, *Work Scholars*

The publication of this book was made possible, in part, by the generous support of The Turner Foundation, Inc.

First edition
Printed in Hong Kong
10 9 8 7 6 5 4 3 2 1

Library of Congress Control Number: 2008939806
ISBN 978-1-59711-091-4

Henry Art Gallery
Sawdust Mountain is copublished with the Henry Art Gallery, University of Washington, Seattle.

Aperture Foundation books are available in North America through:
D.A.P./Distributed Art Publishers
155 Sixth Avenue, 2nd Floor
New York, N.Y. 10013
Phone: (212) 627-1999
Fax: (212) 627-9484

Aperture Foundation books are distributed outside North America by:
Thames & Hudson
181A High Holborn
London WC1V 7QX
United Kingdom
Phone: + 44 20 7845 5000
Fax: + 44 20 7845 5055
Email: sales@thameshudson.co.uk

aperturefoundation
547 West 27th Street
New York, N.Y. 10001
www.aperture.org

The purpose of Aperture Foundation, a non-profit organization, is to advance photography in all its forms and to foster the exchange of ideas among audiences worldwide.